THE ART OF TED WATES

the happy Lowry of Hampshire

Tim Saunders

Tim Saunders Publications

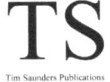

Copyright © 2023 Tim Saunders

All rights reserved

No part of this book may be reproduced, or stored in a retrieval system, or transmitted in any form or by any means, electronic, mechanical, photocopying, recording, or otherwise, without express written permission of the publisher.

Cover design by: Tour de France by Ted Wates (Sold)
www.tedwates.weebly.com

To my family for putting up with me!

Everything has its beauty, but not everyone sees it.

ANDY WARHOL (1928 TO 1987)

CONTENTS

Title Page	
Copyright	
Dedication	
Epigraph	
Poem	1
Introduction	2
Landscapes	3
Inspiration	16
Life	17
Transport	27
Process	36
Sports	37
Sketchbook	49
About The Author	59
Praise For Author	61
Tim Saunders Publications	63

POEM

<u>An artist called Ted</u>

There was an artist called Ted
who had colourful pictures
in his head...
"I live to paint,"
he often said
so prolific,
he couldn't go to bed
but created oils
on canvas instead...
"They could be worth lots,
when I'm dead..."
he mused to his wife
the poor woman, who married Ted...
"As long as it keeps you occupied,
I'm happy," she said.

TA Saunders

INTRODUCTION

Ted Wates - the happy Lowry of Hampshire, is the nom de plume of Tim Saunders, who enjoys painting and making things. He greatly admires LS Lowry and Fred Yates, warming to the childlike simplicity of their paintings. But it is Fred Yates who truly inspires him because of his love of bright, bold colours and what can only be described as his absolutely decadent use of oil paint, applying it thickly and often straight from the tube. Fred painted with his fingers, palette knives and anything that was close to hand, working alla prima. Ted emulates this in his own way and the bulk of his work is in oil paint. It is these paintings that feature in this collector's edition.

Unlike Fred, Ted's preference is to work on postcard size 7" x 5" canvas board. This, he does in order to produce affordable art that doesn't require too much space. For that reason it is only the few paintings he produces that are larger where the sizes are included in this book.

Ted's work is in private collections in England, France and Greece.

Keep up-to-date by visiting tedwates.weebly.com.

Tim Saunders

LANDSCAPES

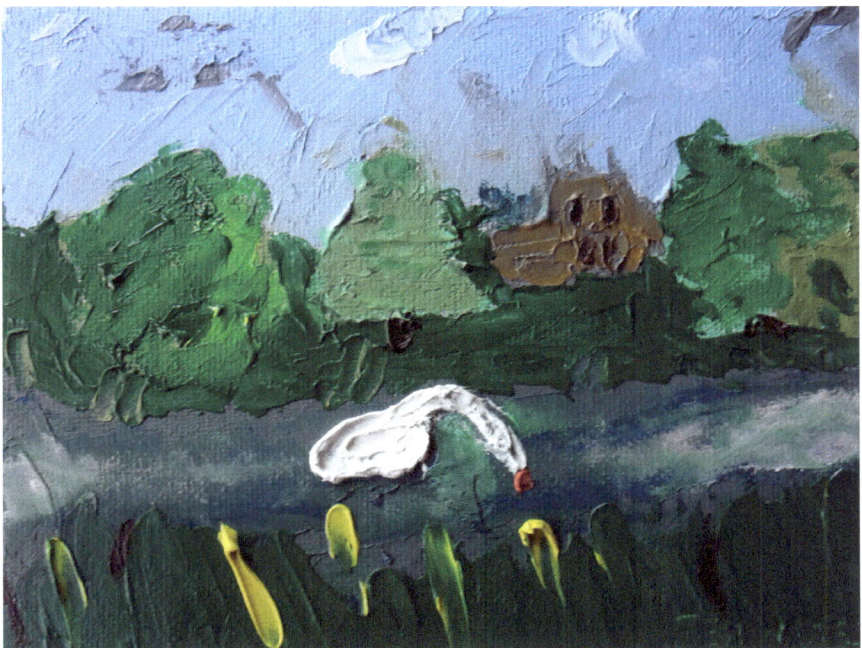

ABOVE: Swan, Sherborne Castle, Dorset

One summer's day my family and I took a trip to Sherborne Castle in Dorset where I saw a majestic swan on the surrounding lake. That was all the inspiration I needed to get my palette knife!

OVERLEAF: Penzance Harbour, Cornwall, 15" x 20"

I love Cornwall, just like Fred Yates did. He lived there for some years. My painting of Penzance Harbour is a wonderful reminder of this fabulous part of the world where we have enjoyed some excellent holidays. This is the largest painting I have so far produced and therefore the most expensive. It happens to be my children's favourite, too. I love the colours and the people make me smile. Oh, it's a fun life and there's never a dull moment here, I can tell you.

TIM SAUNDERS

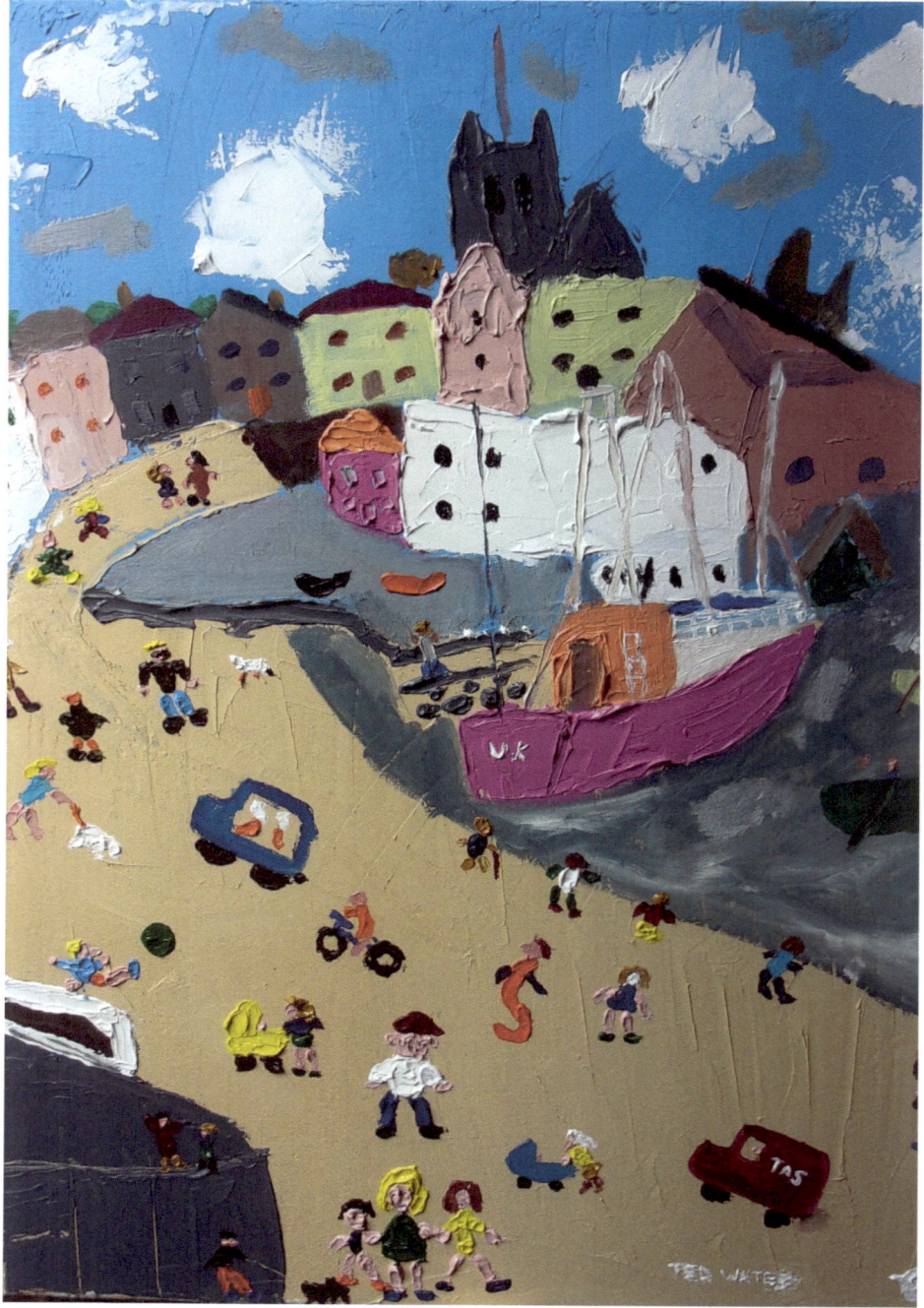

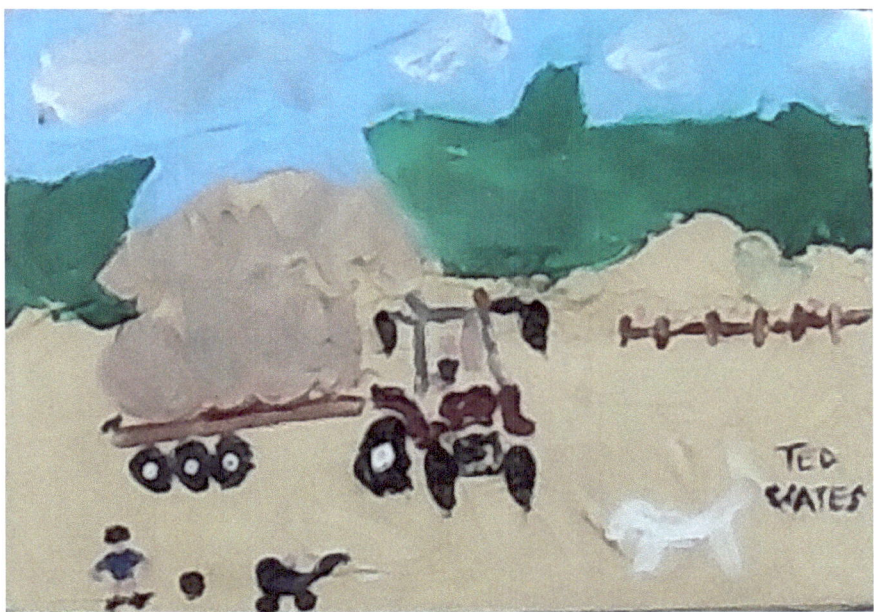

ABOVE: Bringing in the harvest

We were returning from a holiday in Suffolk when to my right I saw this tractor loaded up with hay bales. A quintessential English summer scene.

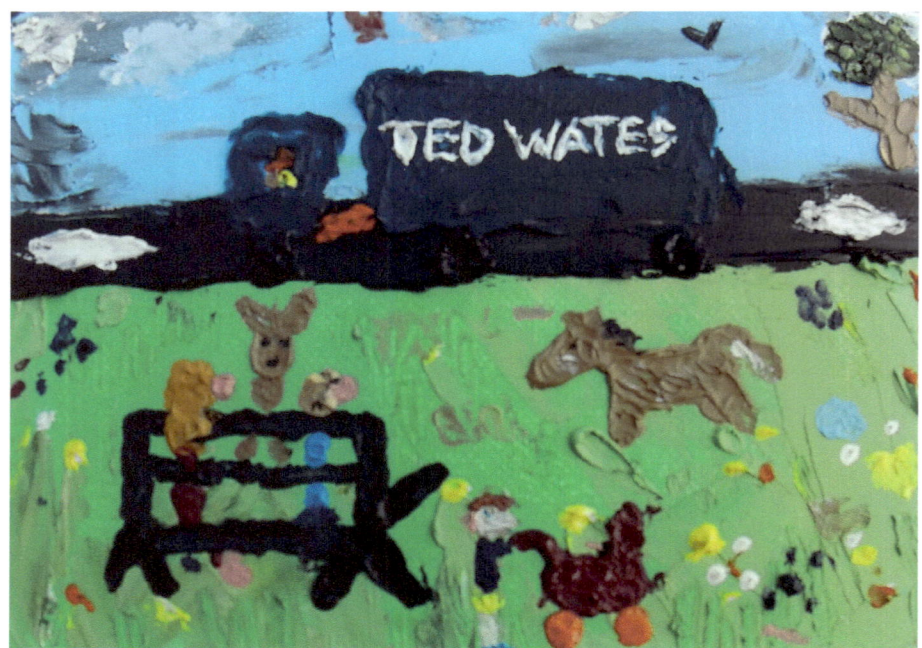

ABOVE: A delivery of Ted Wates paintings makes its way through the New Forest

I am given to wishful thinking and why not? This happy summer scene raises a smile.

THE ART OF TED WATES

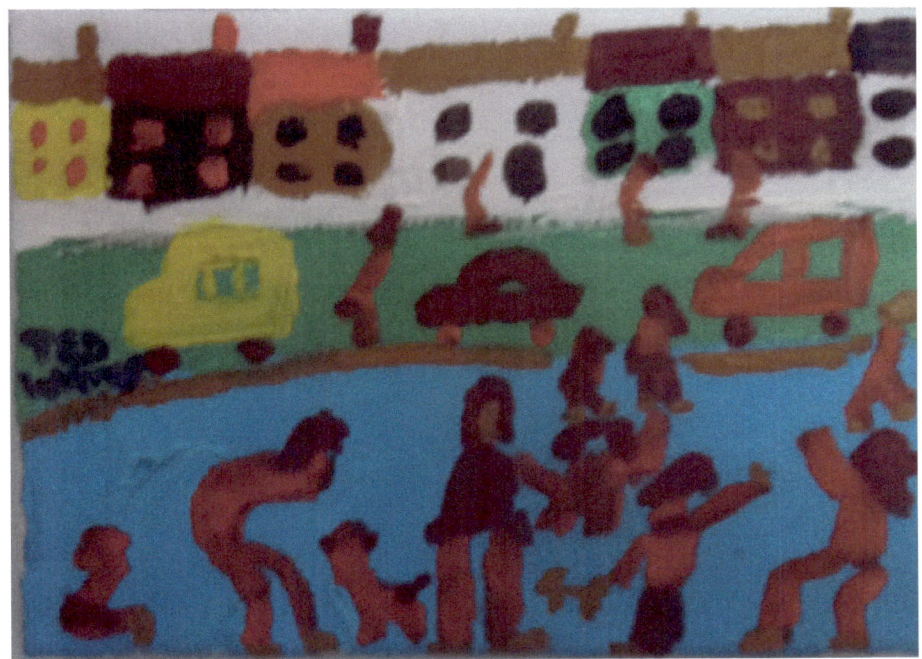

ABOVE: Another busy day (Private collection)

You can see Fred Yates' inspiration here. This, one of my early attempts, hangs in my son's bedroom.

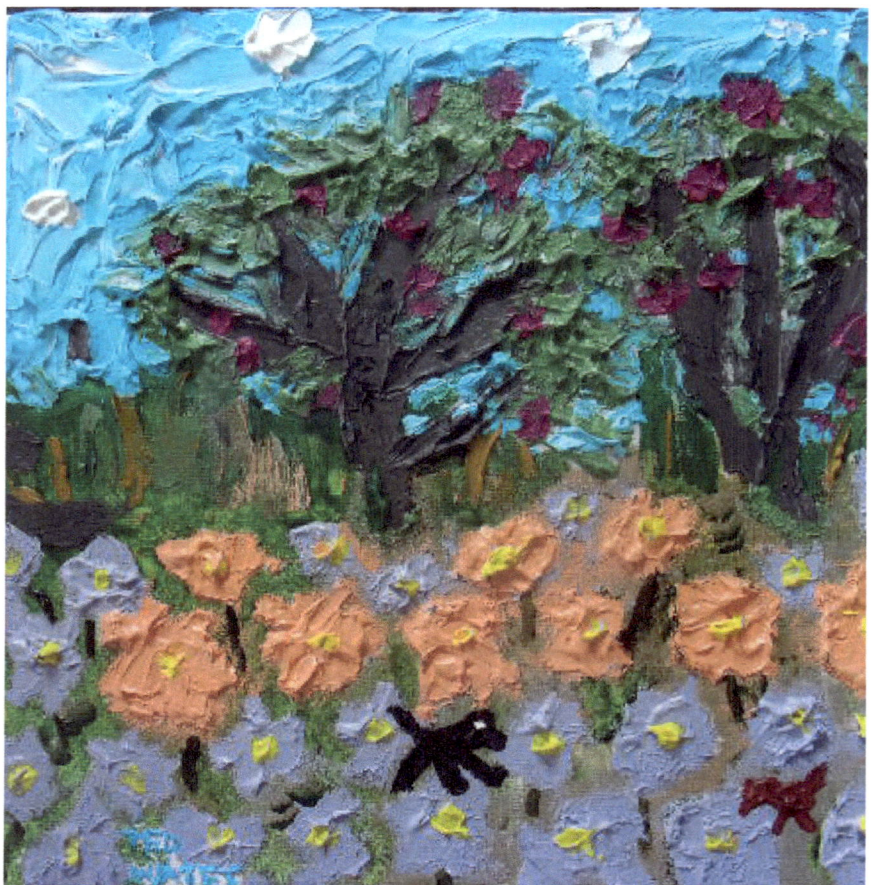

ABOVE: Apple trees and bright flowers

This was an unusual size for me and rather than using canvas on board as I prefer, I used a cut up cereal box.

THE ART OF TED WATES

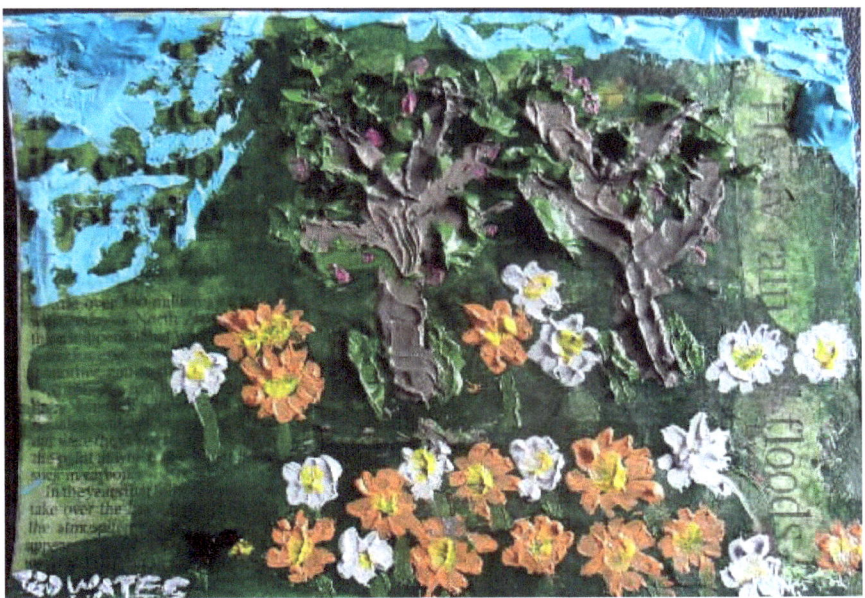

ABOVE: Apple trees and flowers, mixed media, 10.5 x 14.8cm inspired by nature, Nottinghamshire Wildlife Trust entry 2020

I produced this for a charity exhibition in Nottingham during Covid where all works were available for £5. It sold. I used a cut up cereal box for the canvas and incorporated some relevant newspaper cuttings about the environment in the collage.

OVERLEAF: David Blaine and his balloons

In September 2020 famed magician David Blaine jumped from an aeroplane at 20,000 feet clutching balloons. All in a bid to push his limits of survival. He did survive and in so doing inspired me to paint this picture.

TIM SAUNDERS

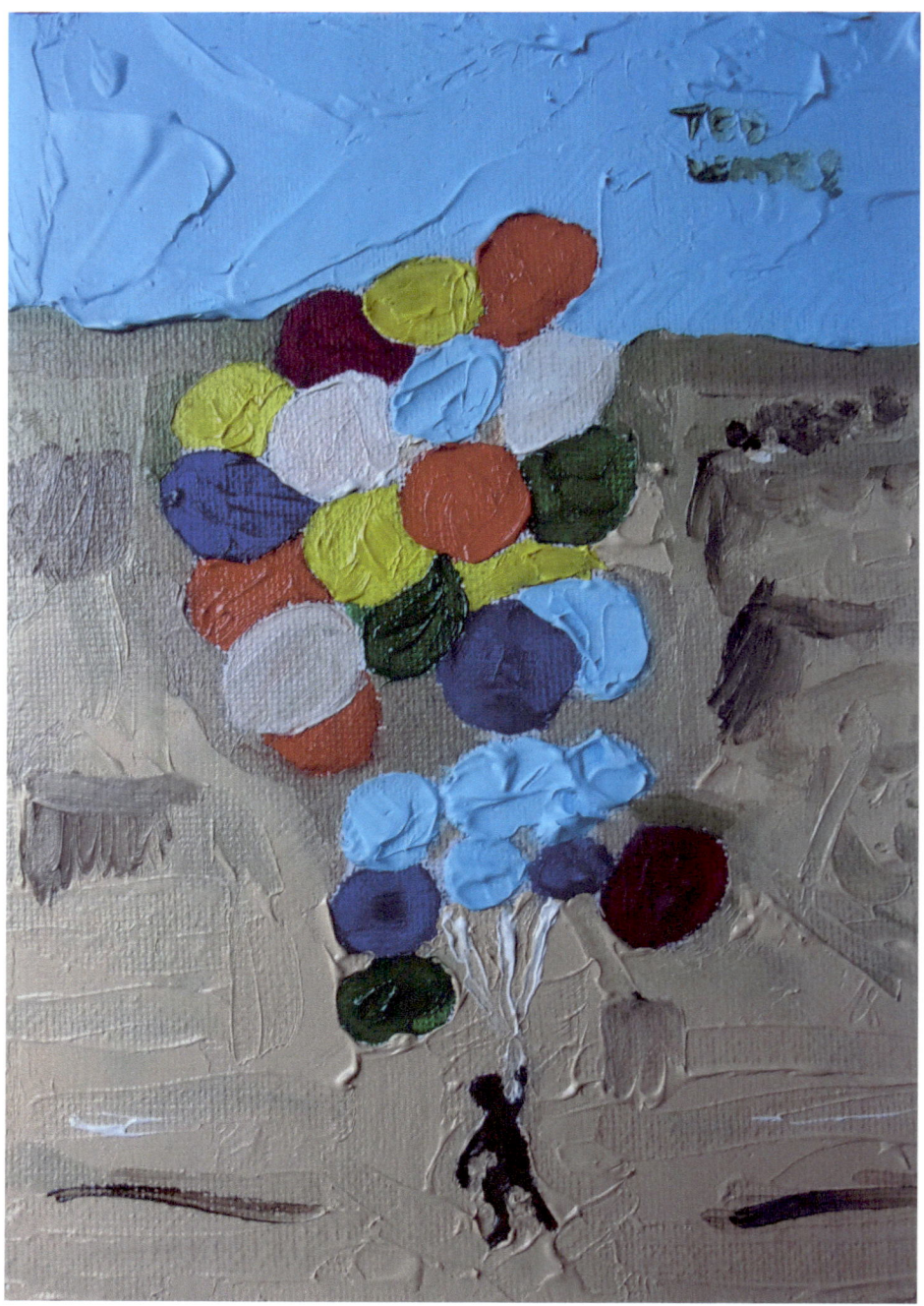

THE ART OF TED WATES

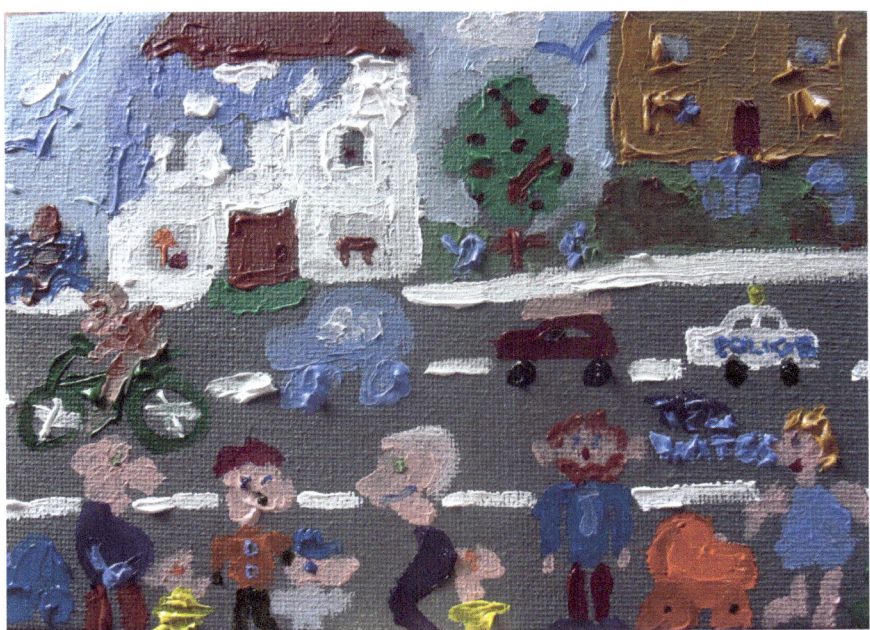

ABOVE: Busy street

"Go on Dad, paint me a picture with a police car in it," demanded my son, Henry, whon was five at the t me. This is the result.

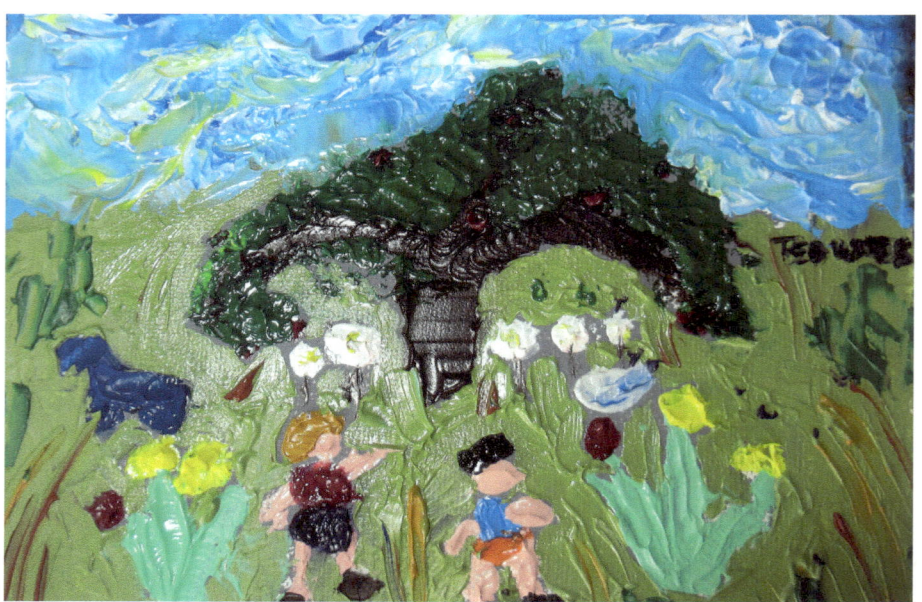

ABOVE: Strolling in the park

Happy days.

THE ART OF TED WATES

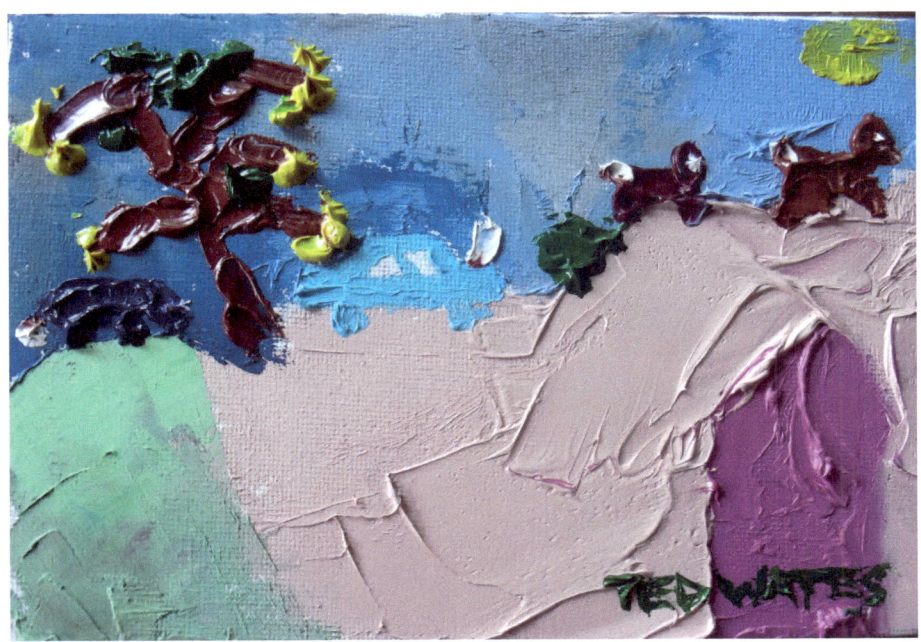

ABOVE: Abstract landscape

This piece was driven by colour and texture, perhaps more so than usual.

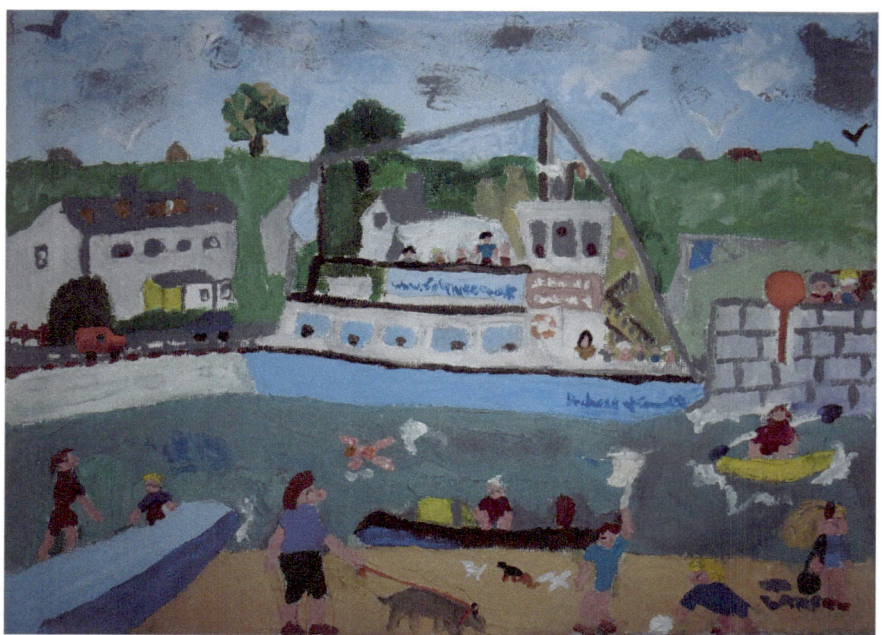

ABOVE: The Duchess of Cornwall, St Mawes ferry, 12" x 9"

Blue is my favourite colour and the shade on this boat really pleases me. This is my second largest painting to date.

THE ART OF TED WATES

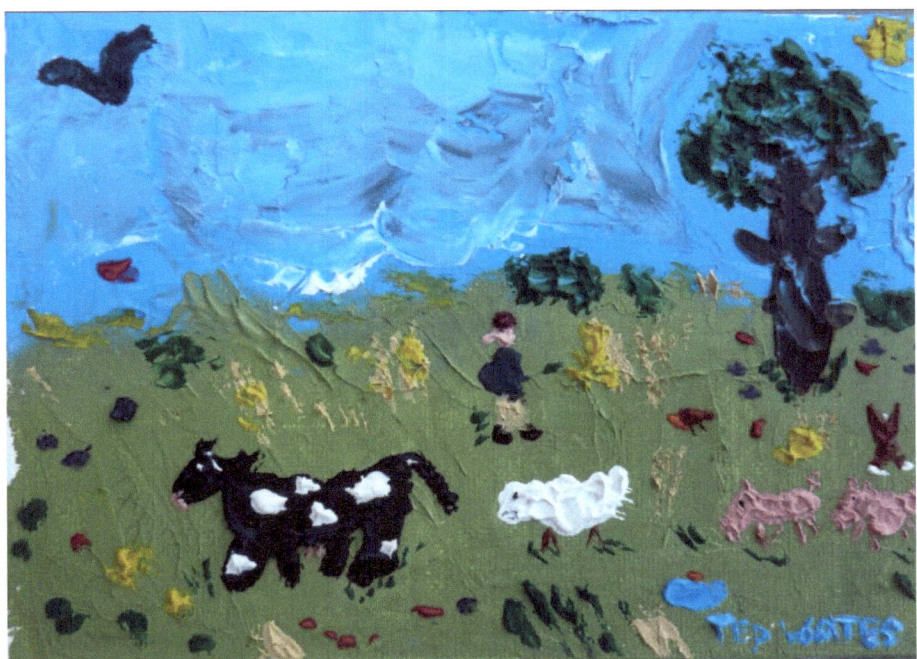

ABOVE: Beautiful English countryside

A celebration.

INSPIRATION

It tends to be the summer months when the weather is good and he can paint outside on the patio, when the works of Ted Wates really come alive. Not many Ted Wates paintings are produced in a year due to time constraints, which makes them all the more exciting. The key is colour, fun and vibrancy. Some are imagined, remembered and others take place right there and then. Occasionally, photographs will be used and sometimes experimentation with collage takes place.

LIFE

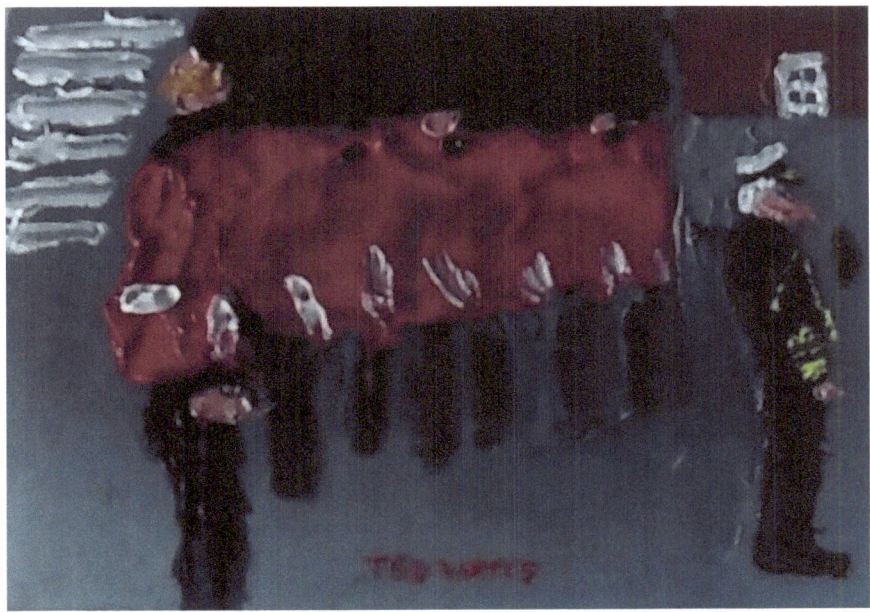

ABOVE: Queen's Guard inspection

I find this a vaguely comical painting because the soldiers are facing in the opposite direction to the commanding officer. I like the contrasting colours.

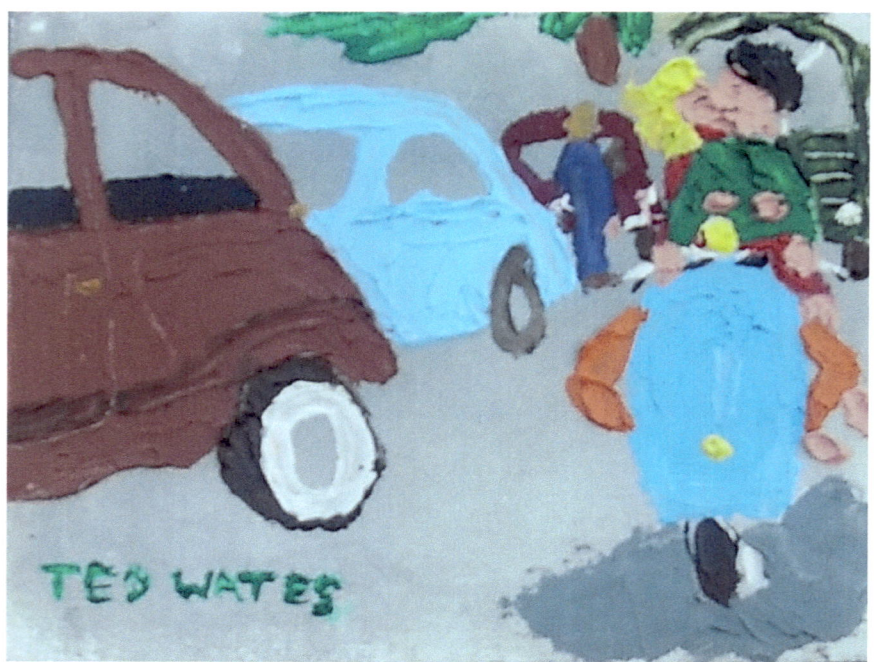

ABOVE\: *Romance in Rome*

I love this painting. Italian design, love in the air, great weather, a bit of action. Great. The colours are just right, too, I think.

OVERLEAF: *Ted Wates self-portrait SOLD to a collector in Greece*

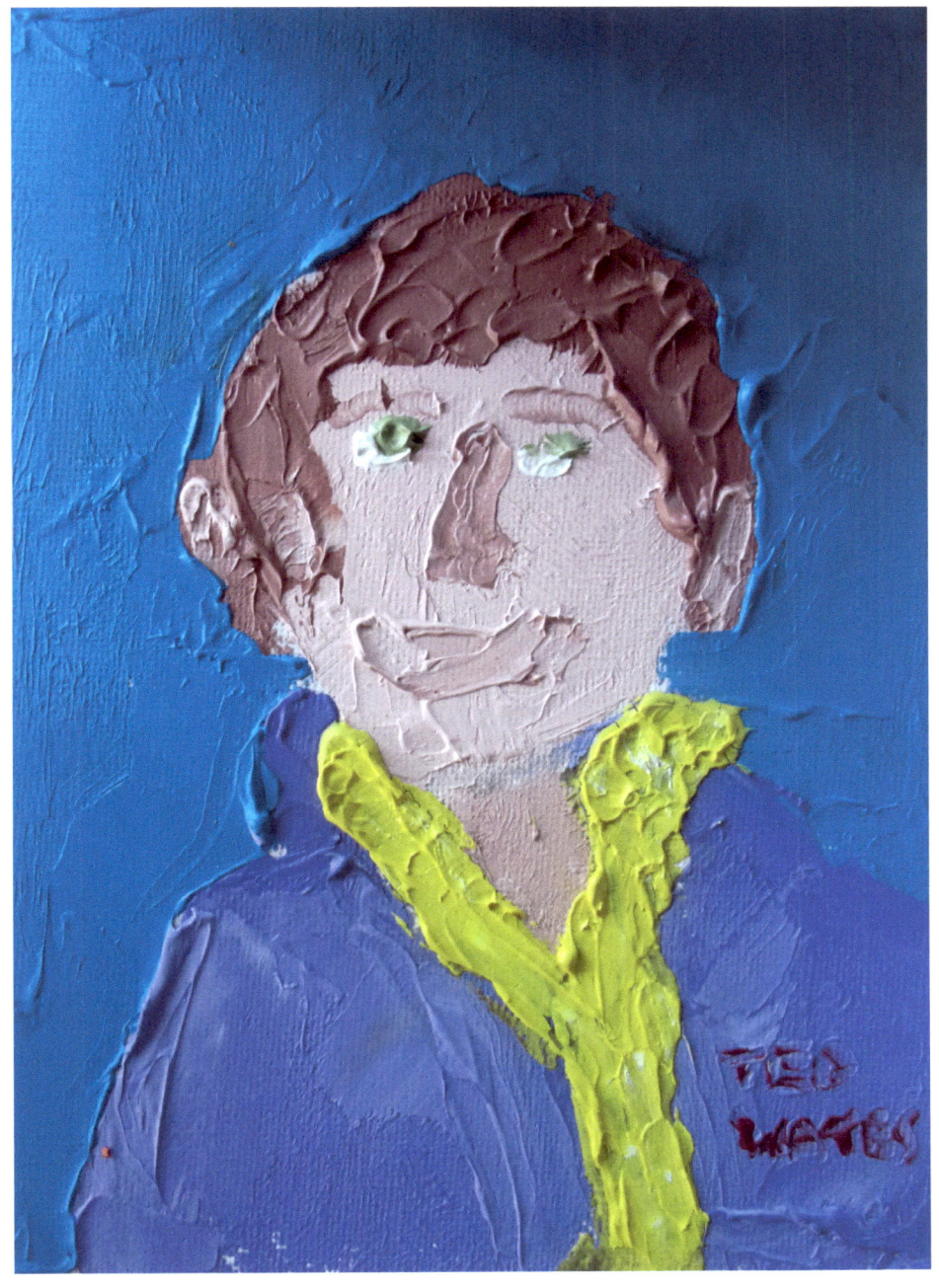

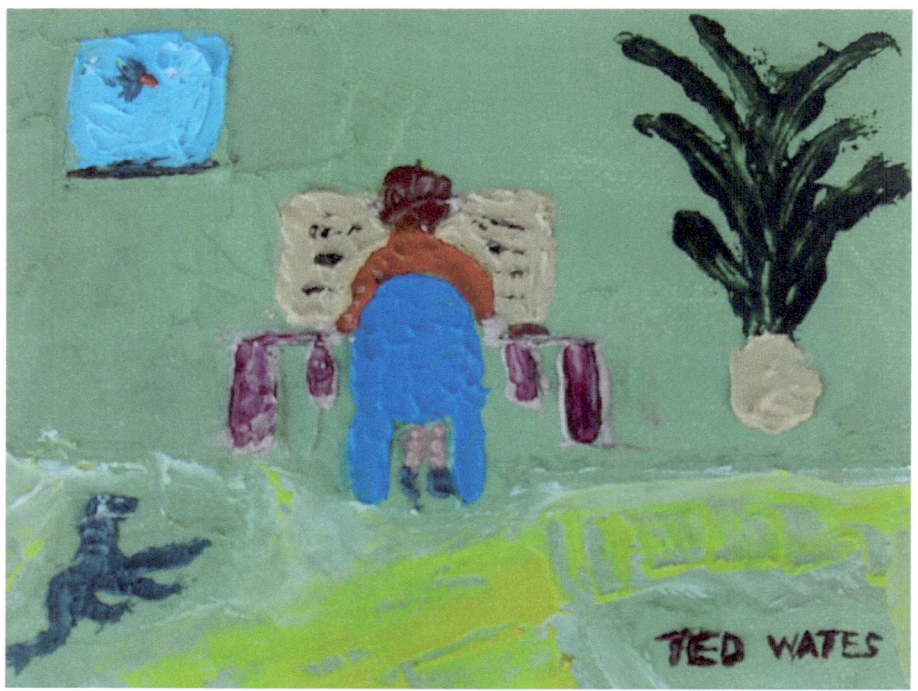

ABOVE: Looking back: Working from home

Looking at the back of things interests me.

THE ART OF TED WATES

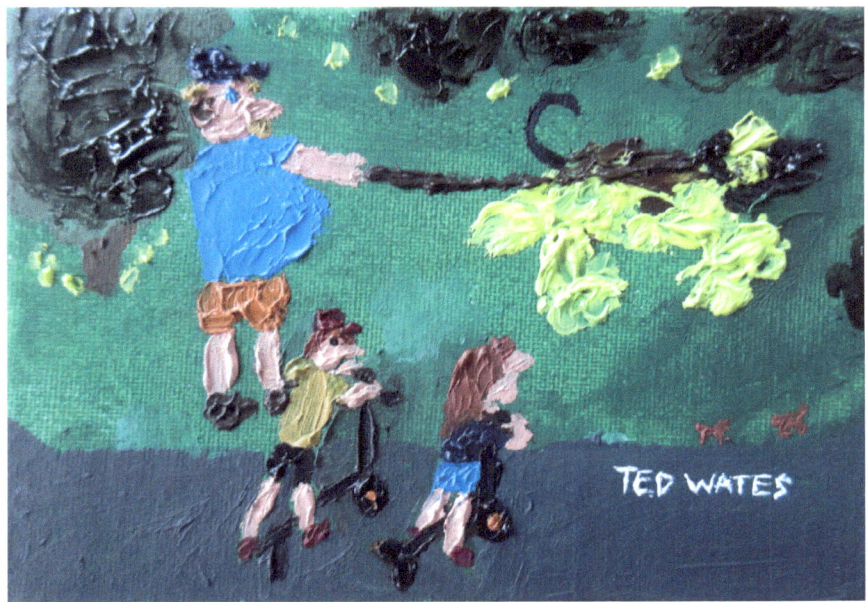

ABOVE: *The day we saw an Afghan Hound (Private collection)*

Heidi, Henry and I were strolling through the park when we saw this sight. We were mesmerised. The Afghan Hound just reminded us of What a Mess and was crying out to be painted.

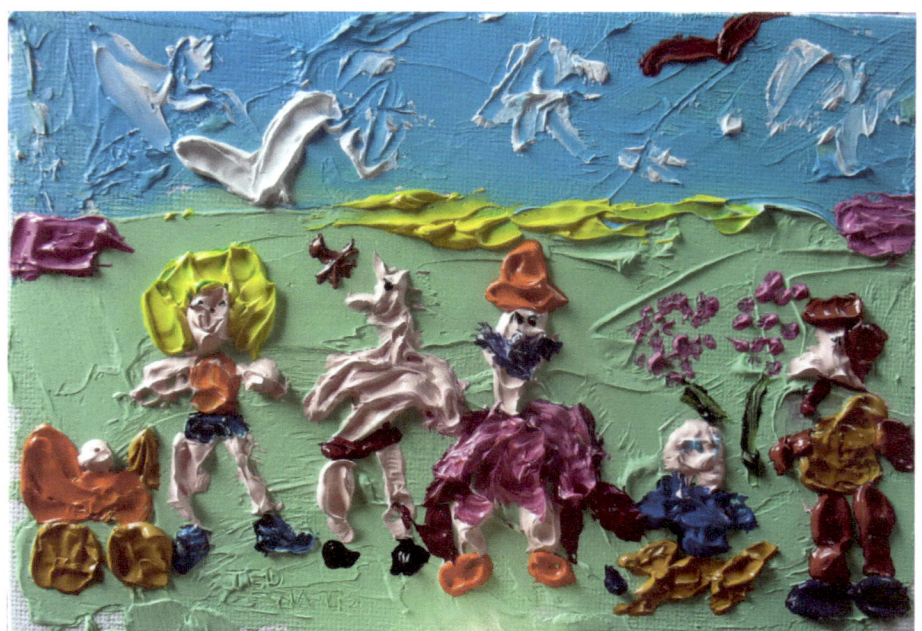

ABOVE: Summer outing

Thick lashings of bright oils. That's what I like.

THE ART OF TED WATES

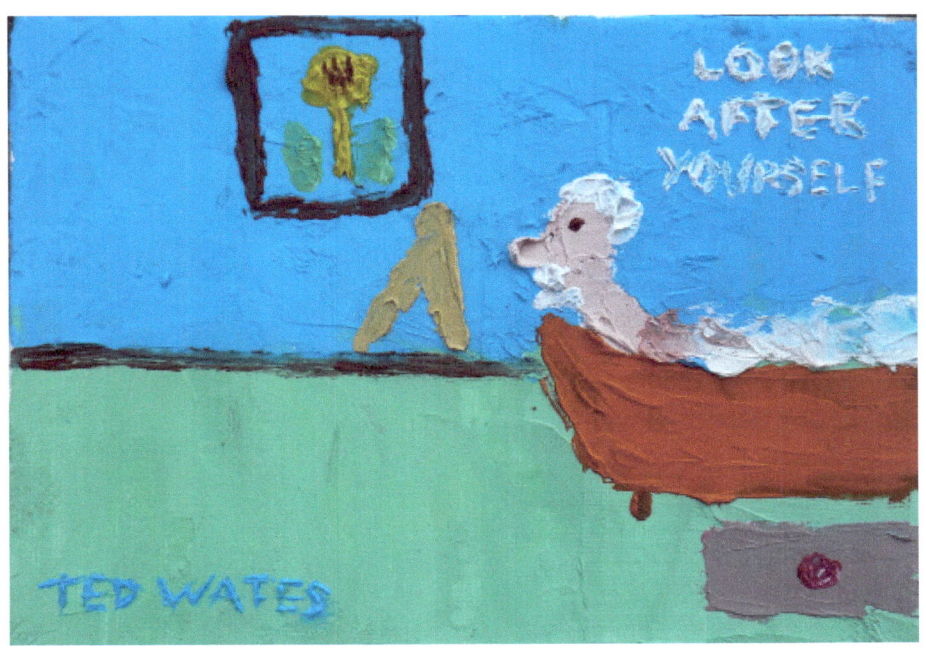

ABOVE: Look after yourself

TIM SAUNDERS

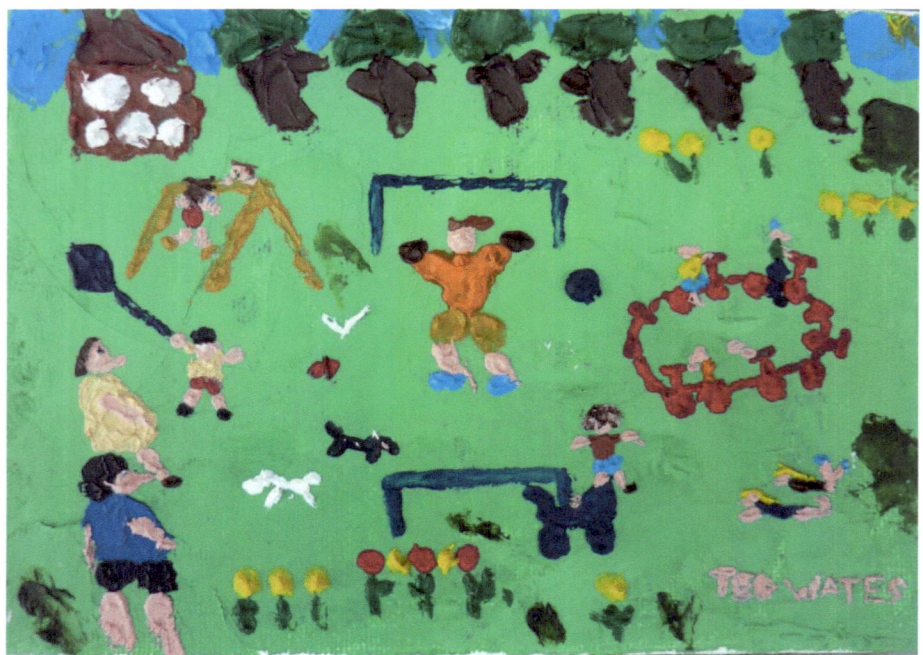

ABOVE: At the park

We go to lots of parks with our children so I can't help but paint them.

THE ART OF TED WATES

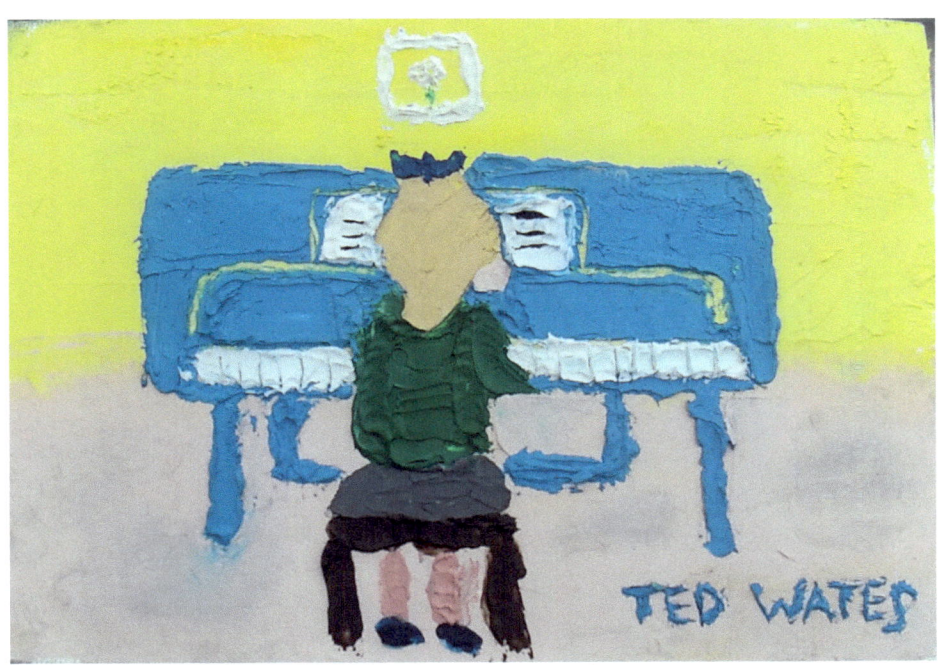

ABOVE: Playing the Joanna
Daughter Heidi (10) inspired me to paint this picture of her playing the piano, early one morning. We have an ebonised piano, which, while fine in the sitting room, is too dark for a Ted Wates painting, so I mixed a lightish blue, which works well, I think. This picture is part of my Looking Back series.

OVERLEAF: Pogoing
Heidi has once again inspired this painting. She's always doing something and on this splendid summer's day she has decided to go on her pogo stick in the garden where we have some really lovely daisies.

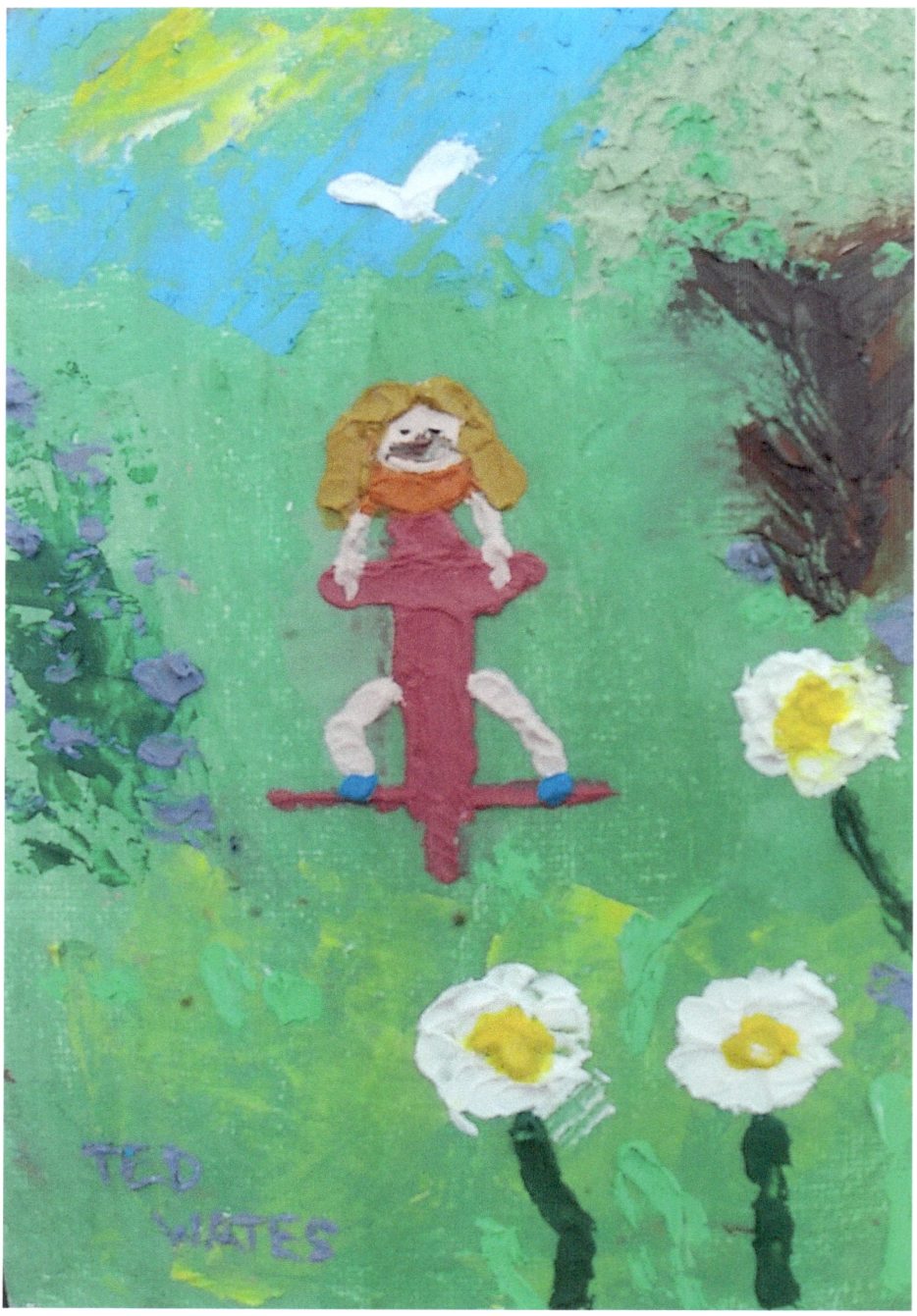

TRANSPORT

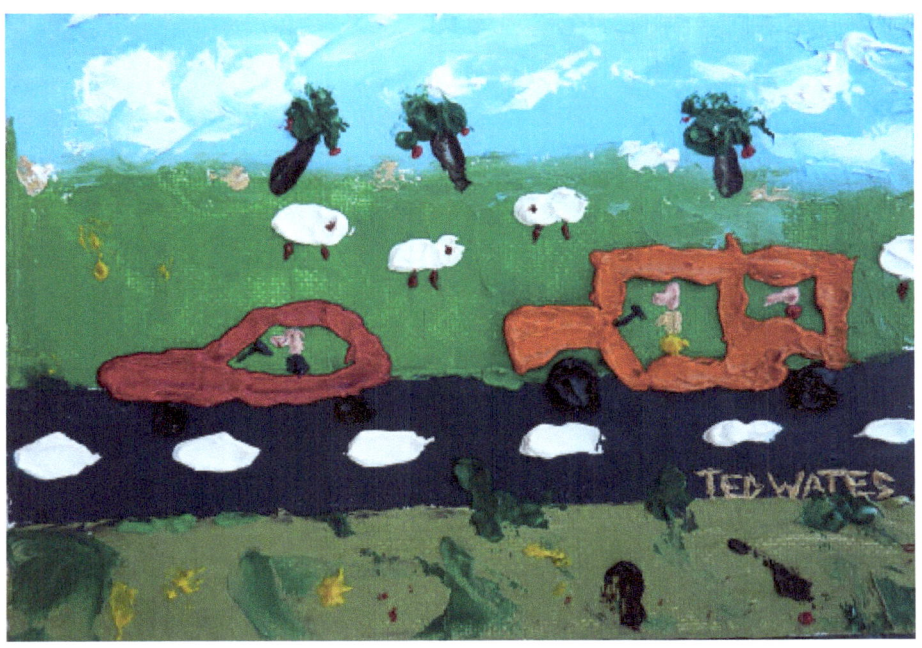

ABOVE: A Jaguar E-Type and a Hummer travel through the English countryside

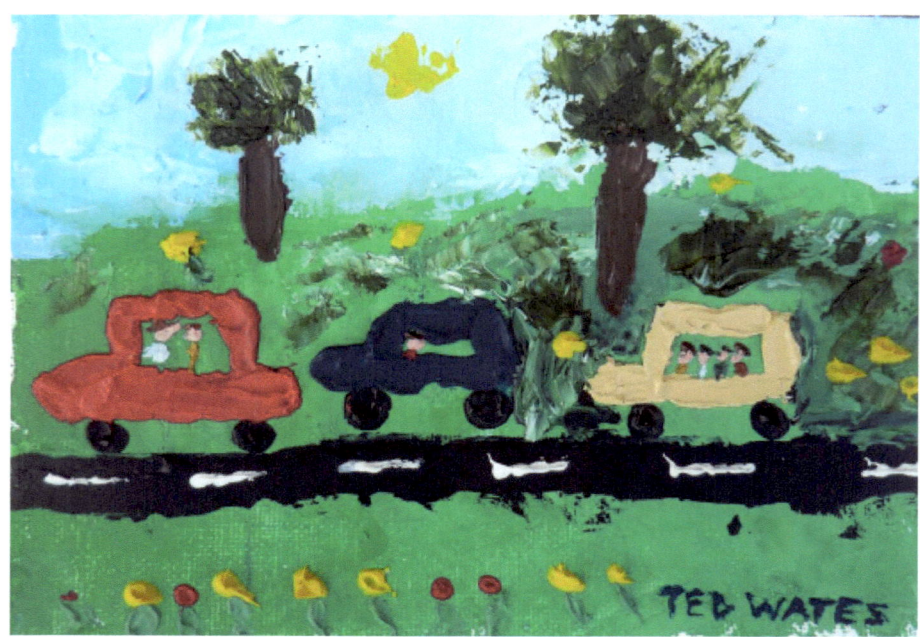

ABOVE: *Nose to tail*

Roadworks in the New Forest cause mayhem during the holiday getaway.

OVERLEAF: *VW Camper at the Warsash Festival (Private collection)*

My favourite blue again.

THE ART OF TED WATES

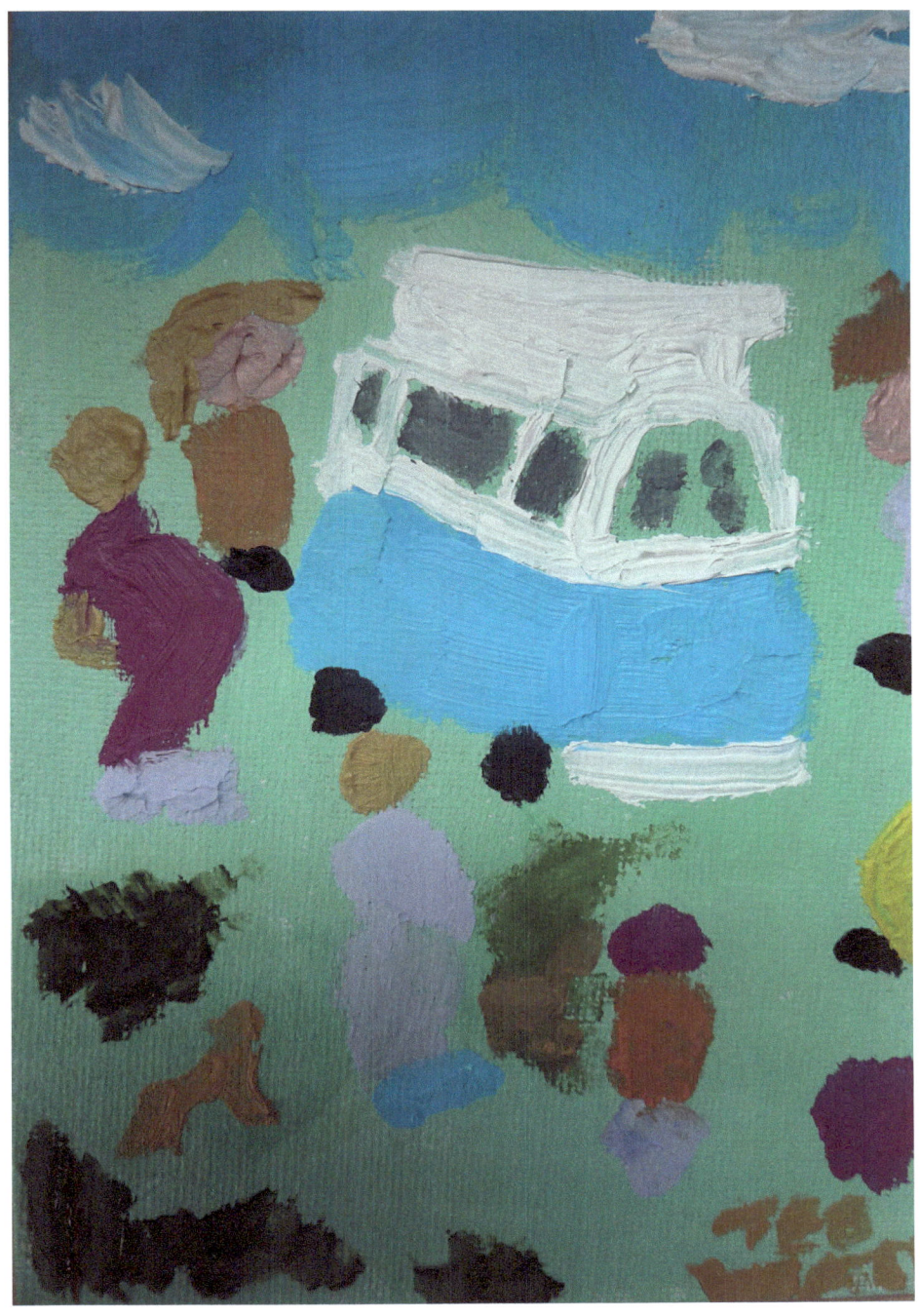

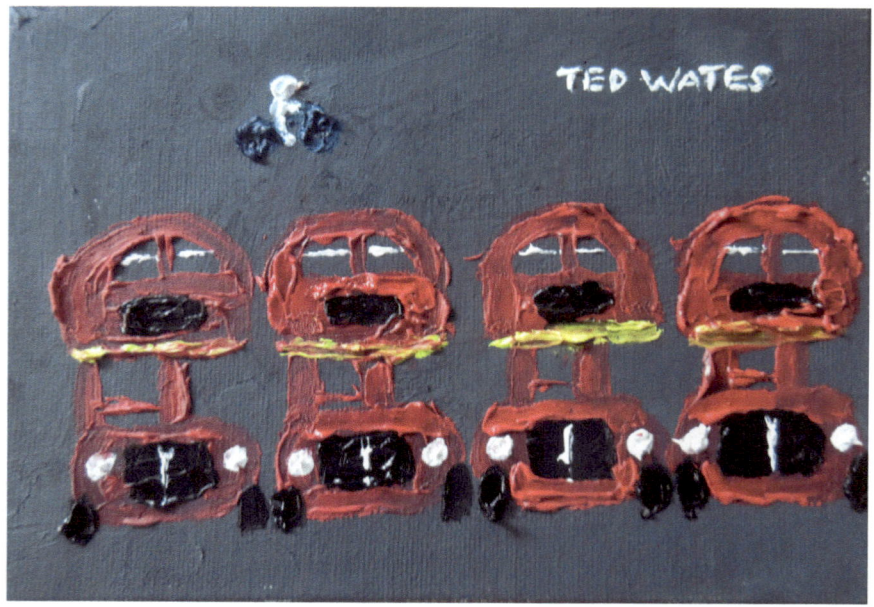

ABOVE: *Evel Knievel (Private collection)*

Evel Knievel attempted to jump 13 London buses at Wembley Stadium in 1975 but failed and crashed in front of 90,000 people fracturing his pelvis and breaking his hand.

OVERLEAF: *Looking back: Front loading dumper*

As I returned from the school run I looked in my rear view mirror and saw a front loading dumper making its way down the road loaded with traffic cones and fencing. That got my creative juices flowing and has inspired a new series of work. I'm drawn to the unusual.

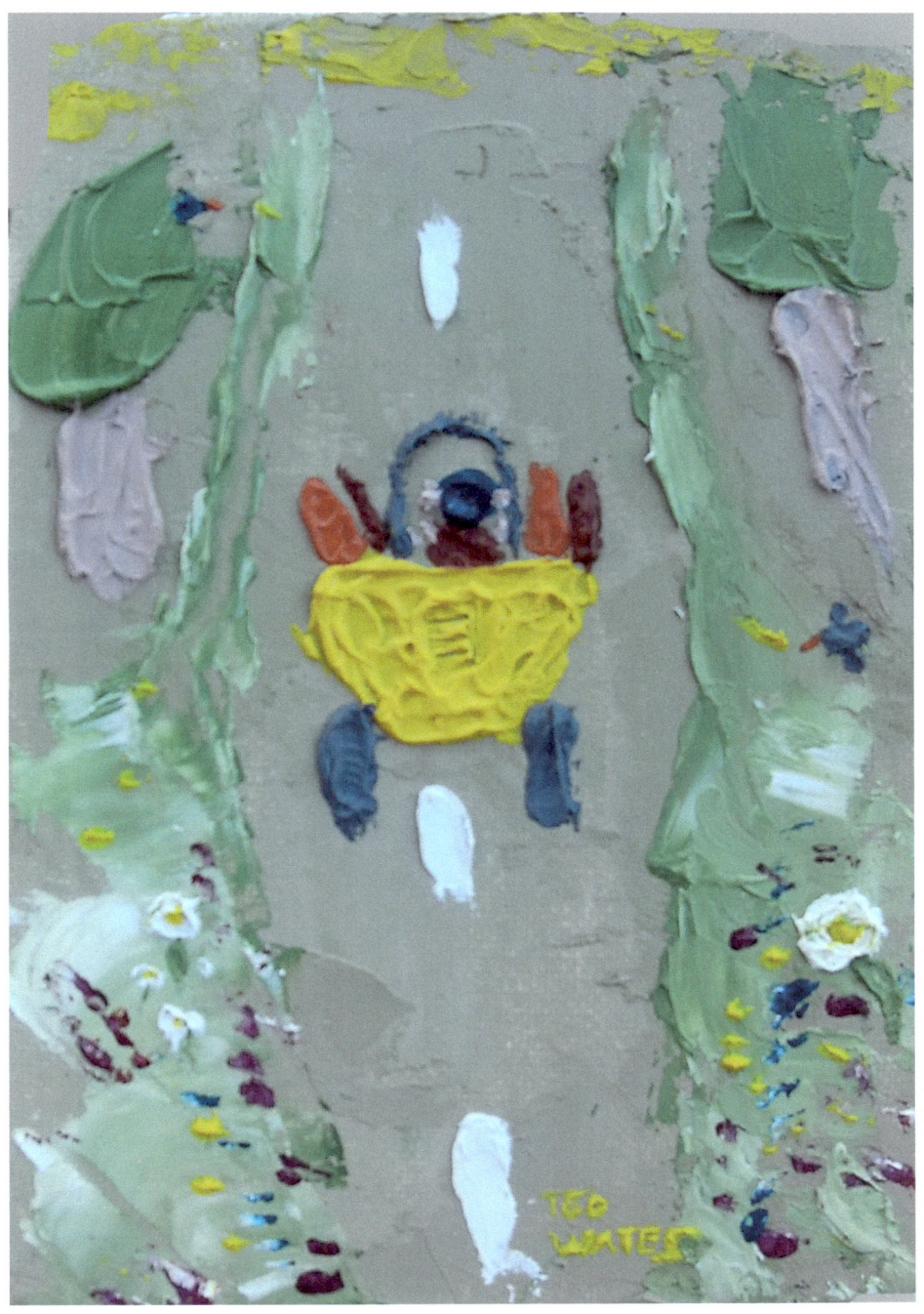

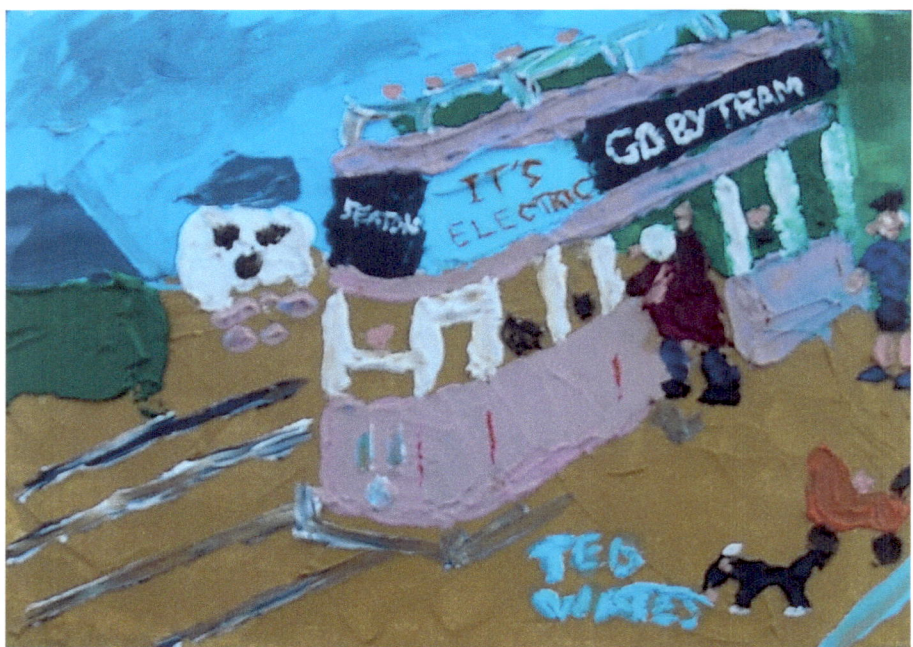

ABOVE: Pink Seaton tram (Private collection)

Seaton has always been a great day out for us and the trams have inspired various paintings.

OVERLEAF: Seaton tram (Private collection)

THE ART OF TED WATES

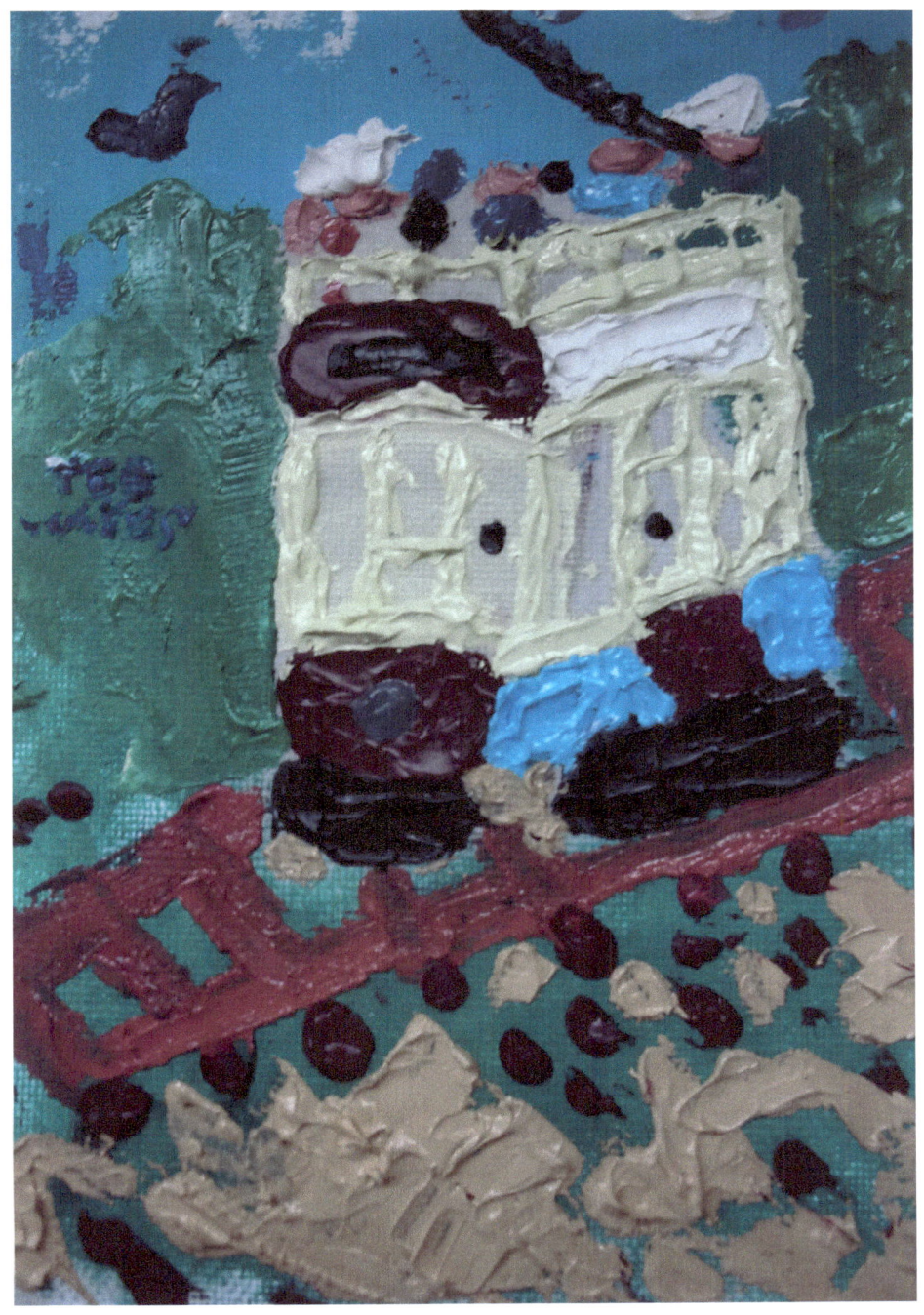

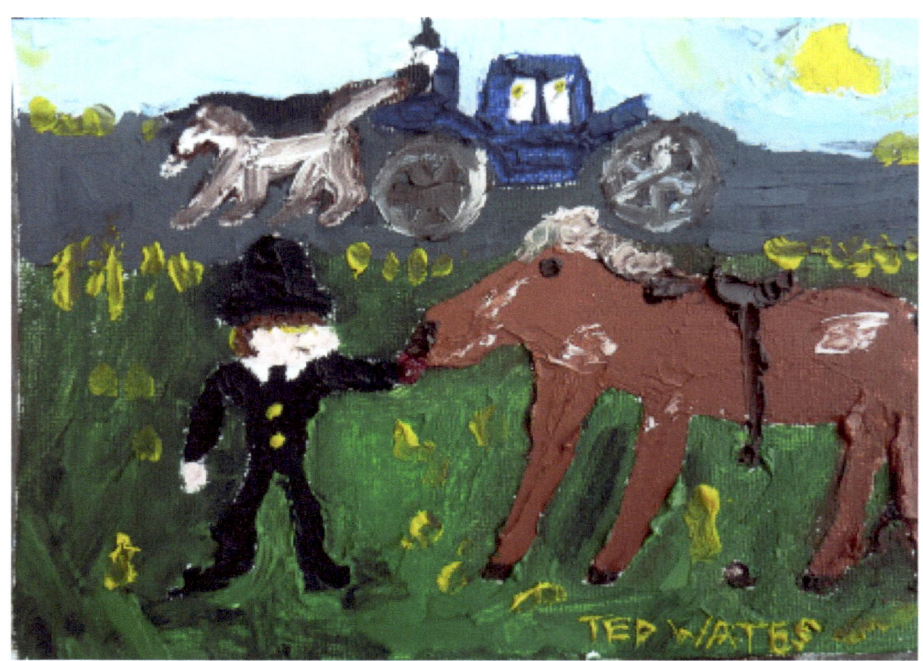

ABOVE: *Eighteenth century Ted*

A nod to the past.

THE ART OF TED WATES

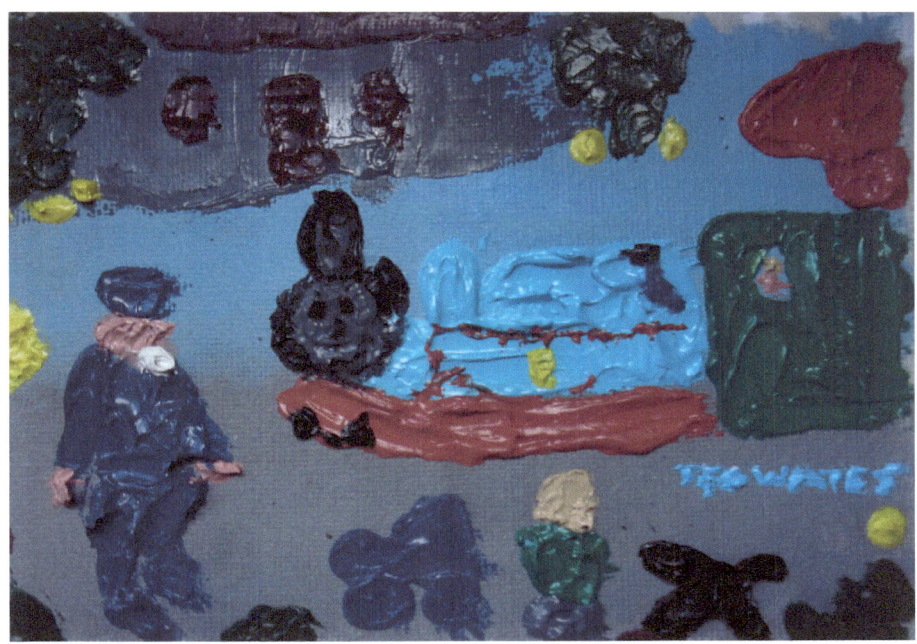

ABOVE: Thomas the Tank Engiine (Private collection)

We visited The Watercress Line in Alton and saw Thomas. Just had to paint him.

PROCESS

There's always incubation and when there's a spark, Ted will dash for his palette knives, brushes and canvas. He's not particular about brands but does insist on having good quality oil paints, typically Winsor & Newton and Rowney. White is a staple of his work with many colours mixed with a dash of it or oodles depending on the shade he's after. It's all great fun and that's what lies behind each of his pictures. Ted doesn't like cleaning up after himself and does enjoy making a mess. His metal palette is covered in much dried paint from previous sessions but he prefers it this way because it means he doesn't use turps to clean up. He doesn't even use turps to clean his brushes or palette knives. Just a bit of tissue suffices. It's better for the environment, he thinks. Knowing when to stop can be tricky but he knows his own mind.

SPORTS

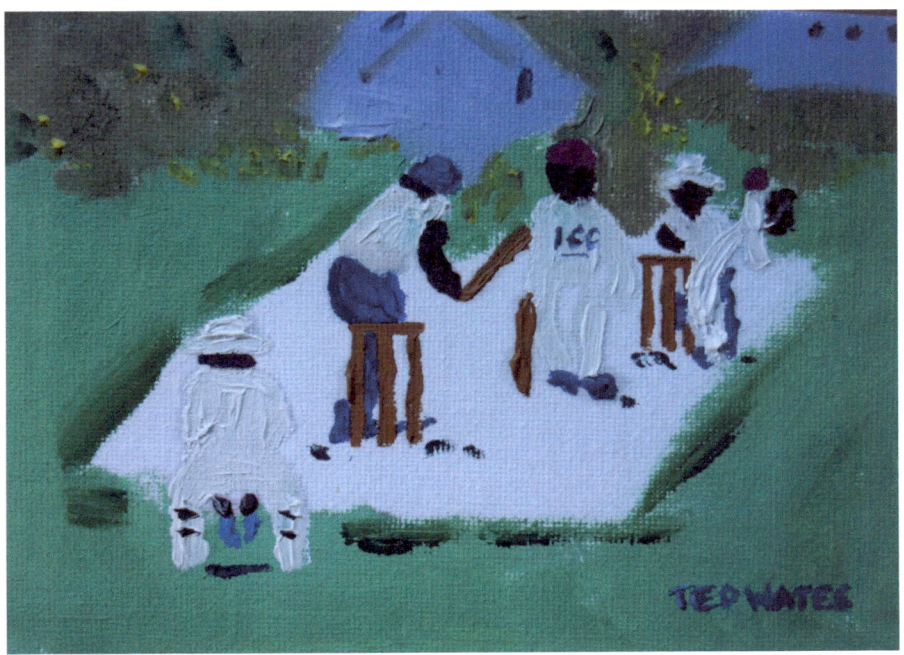

ABOVE: Cricket match SOLD

It was summer and inspired by the sound of leather on willow I fetched my paints. A cricket lover in England bought this one.

TIM SAUNDERS

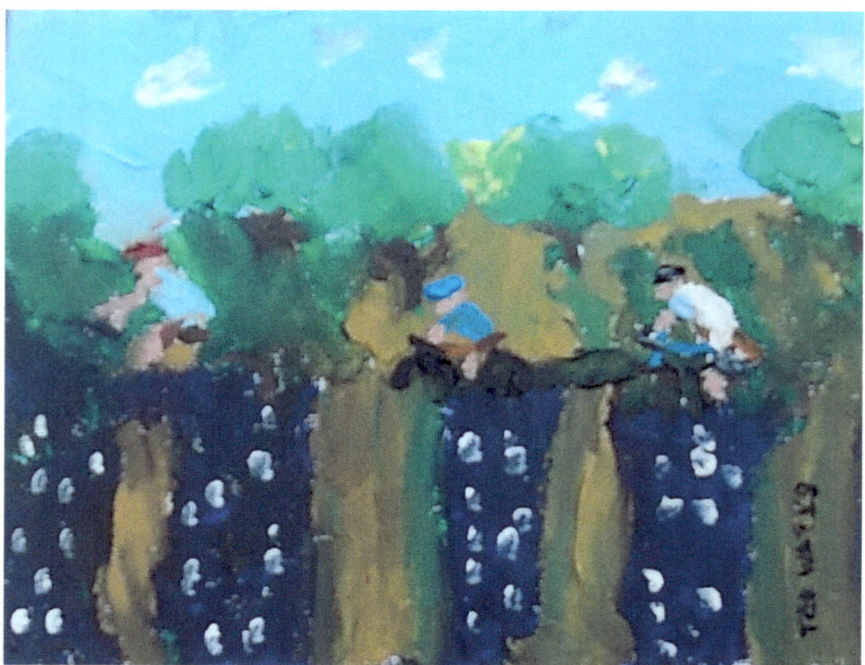

ABOVE: Cycling in Provence

I love lavender fields and when I saw these cyclists I thought it made a great composition. So much of my work is inspired by the summer. It's a season that lifts the spirits.

OVERLEAF: A member of the Household Cavalry, more used to ceremonial duties in London, takes a tumble on the first day of its summer camp in Norfolk. SOLD.

I like a bit of action in a painting.

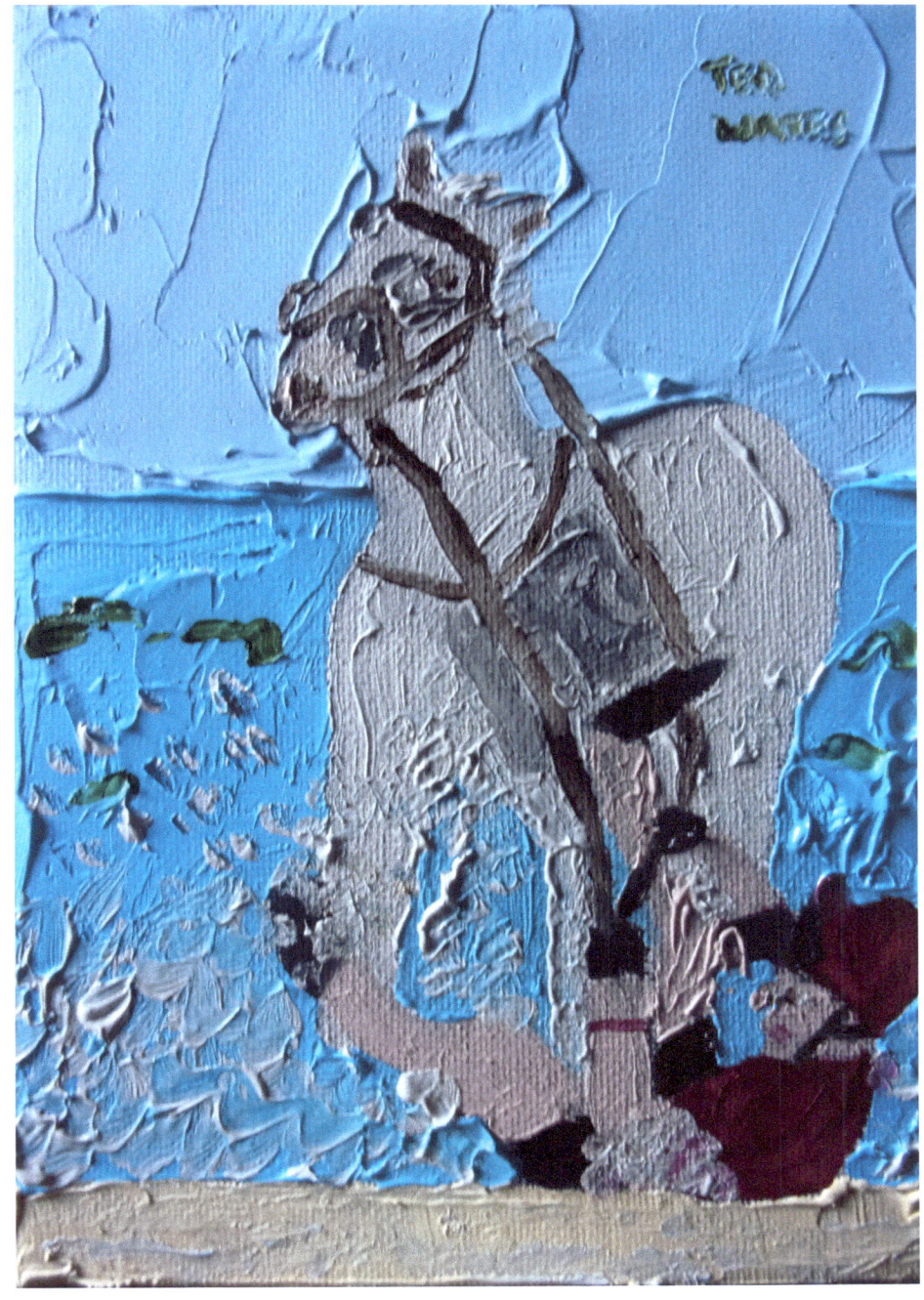

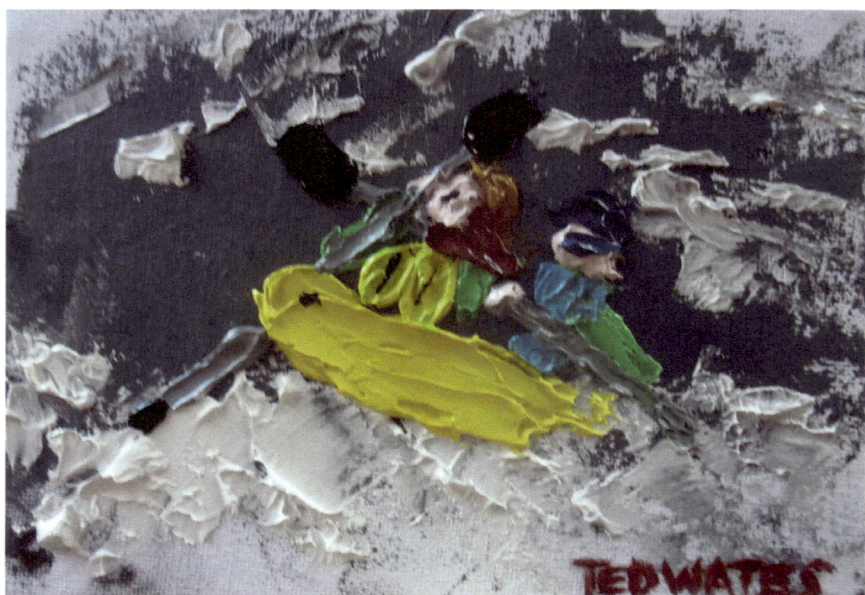

ABOVE: Kayaking

That desire to be doing something, keeping busy, finds me drawn to action. These kayakers are having to work hard in choppy waters.

THE ART OF TED WATES

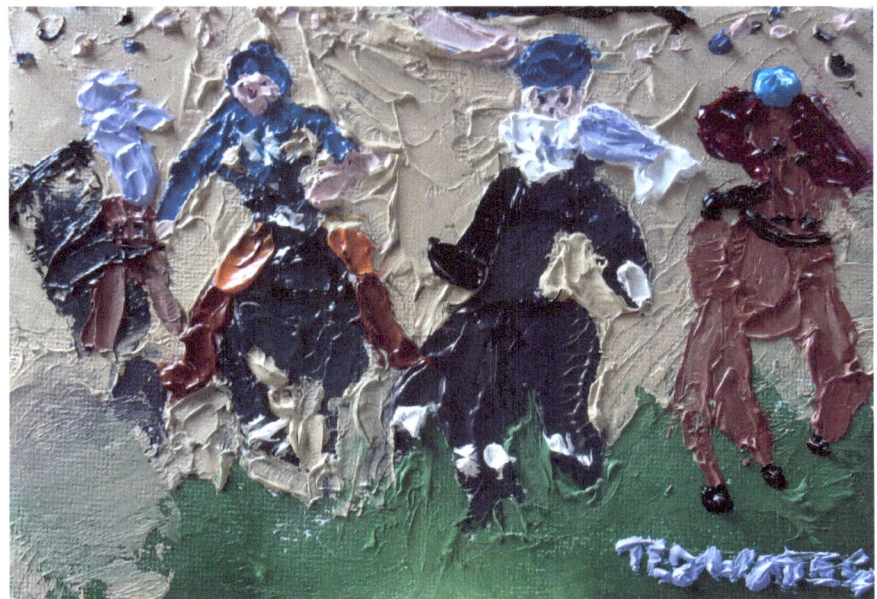

ABOVE: *Horse racing*

Heart in the mouth stuff. Three jockeys battle it out. Who will win? You can sense the adrenalin and the determination in this picture.

TIM SAUNDERS

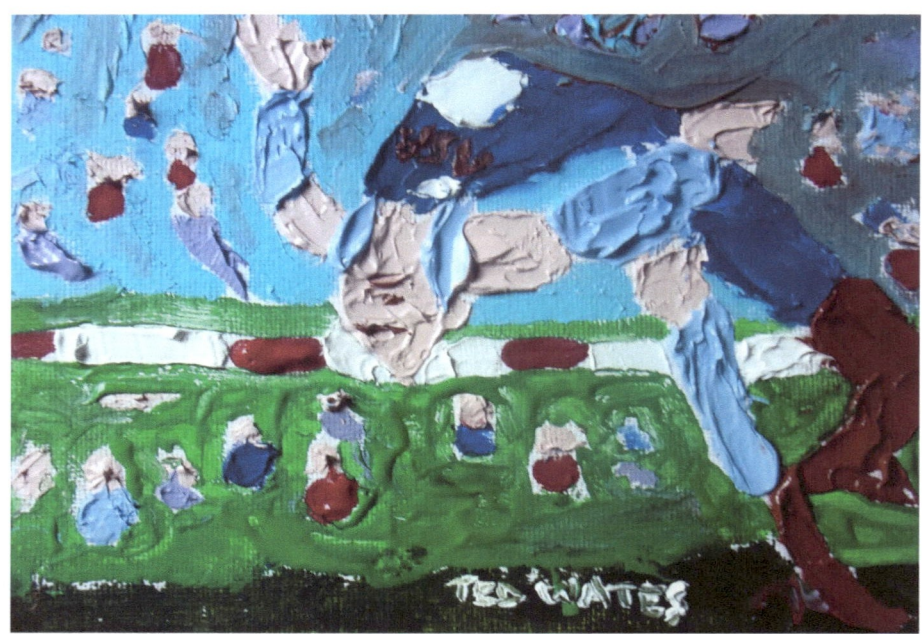

ABOVE: *Paralympics high jump*

For me sport makes great paintings.

THE ART OF TED WATES

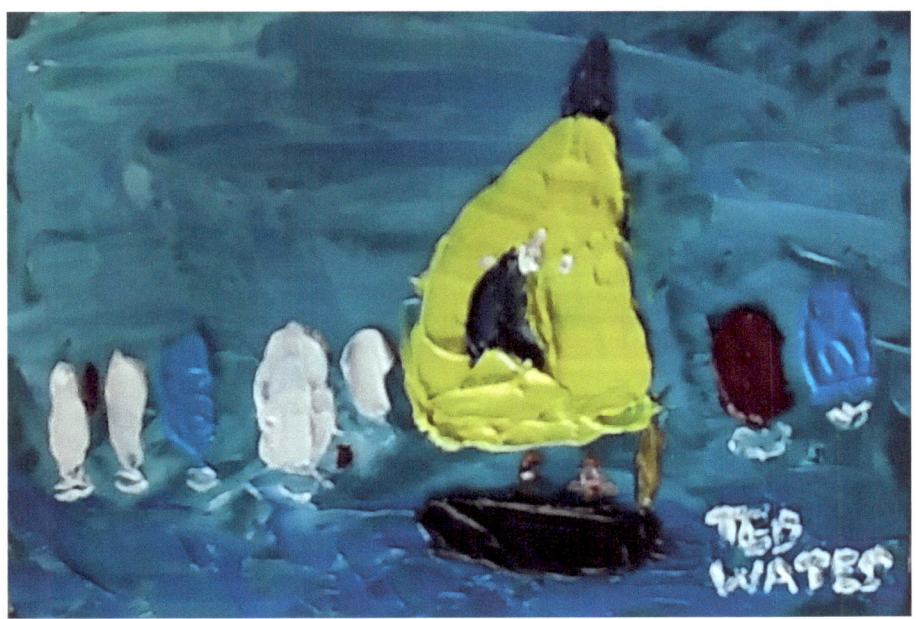

ABOVE: Sailing off the Isle of Wight

What a lovely sight. Another typical British summer scene.

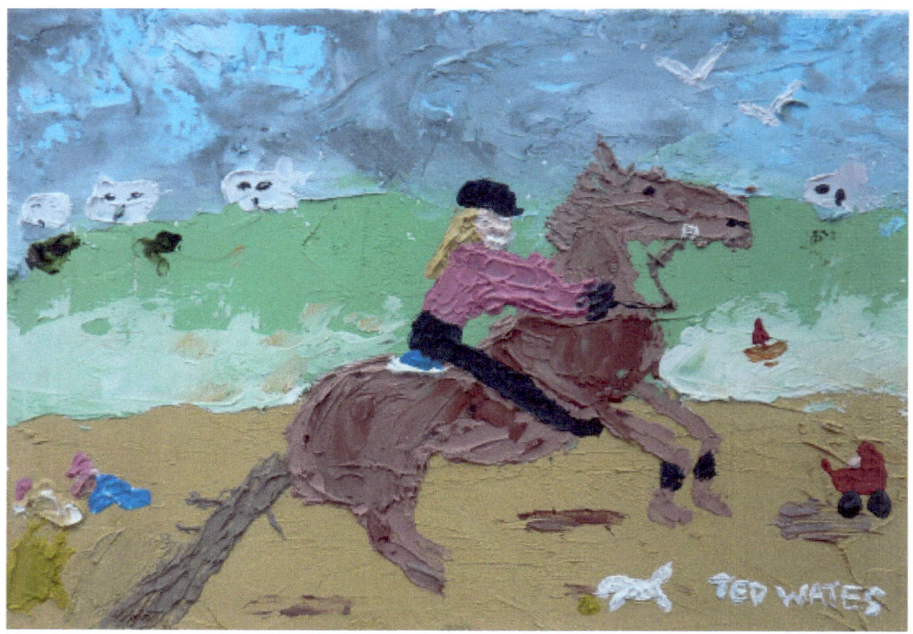

ABOVE: Ride like the wind

My trademark prams, dogs and birds enhance a picture, I think.

THE ART OF TED WATES

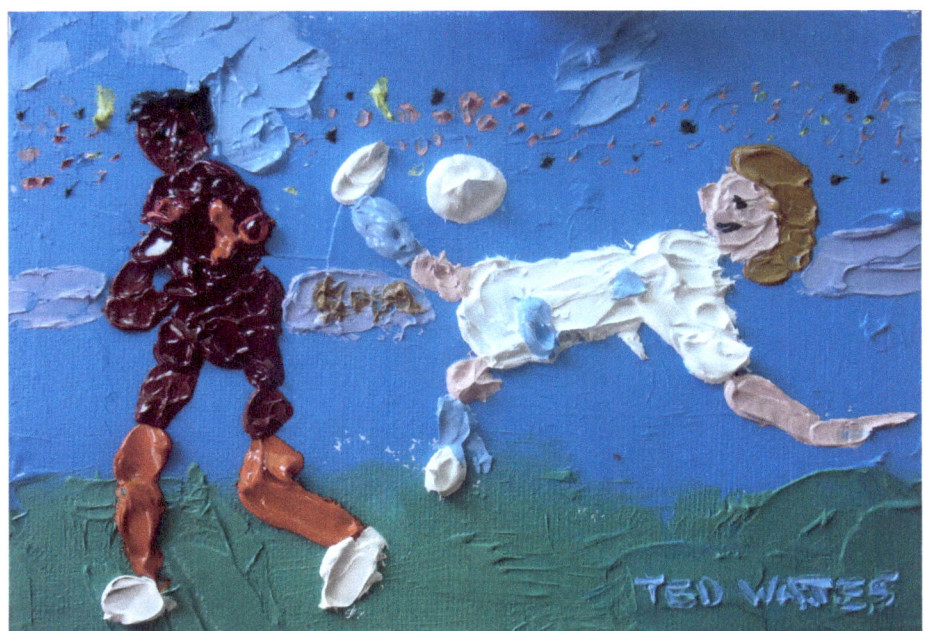

ABOVE: Playing football

This painting is inspired my little son Henry (7), who lives to play football. He always has to be kicking a ball or a stone wherever he walks whether it is down a footpath or in the grounds of a stately home. Great for ball control. As the Captain of Locks Heath Lions U7s he attends regular training sessions and home and away matches. His sheer determination is admirable.

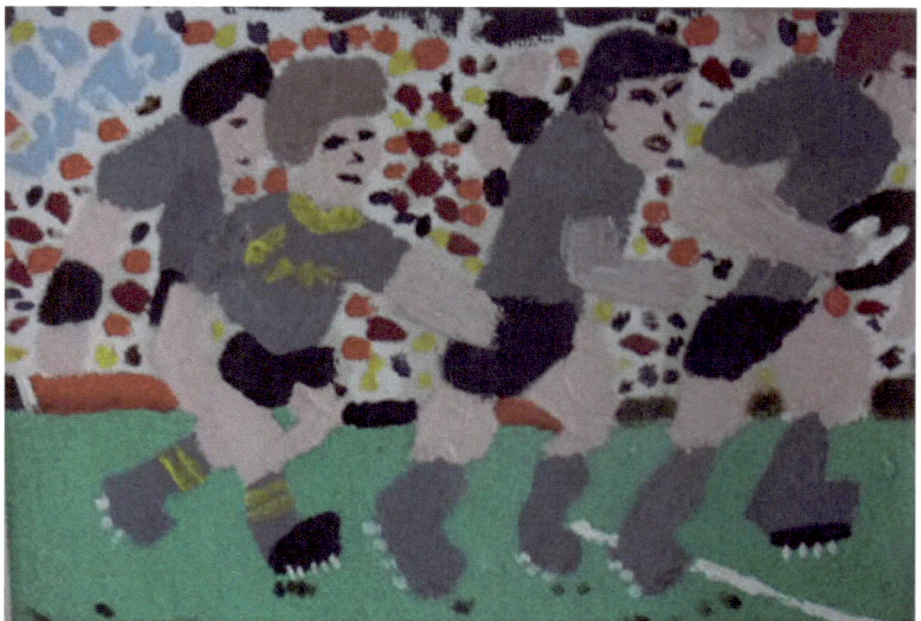

ABOVE: Playing rugby

I was drawn to the action of this sport.

THE ART OF TED WATES

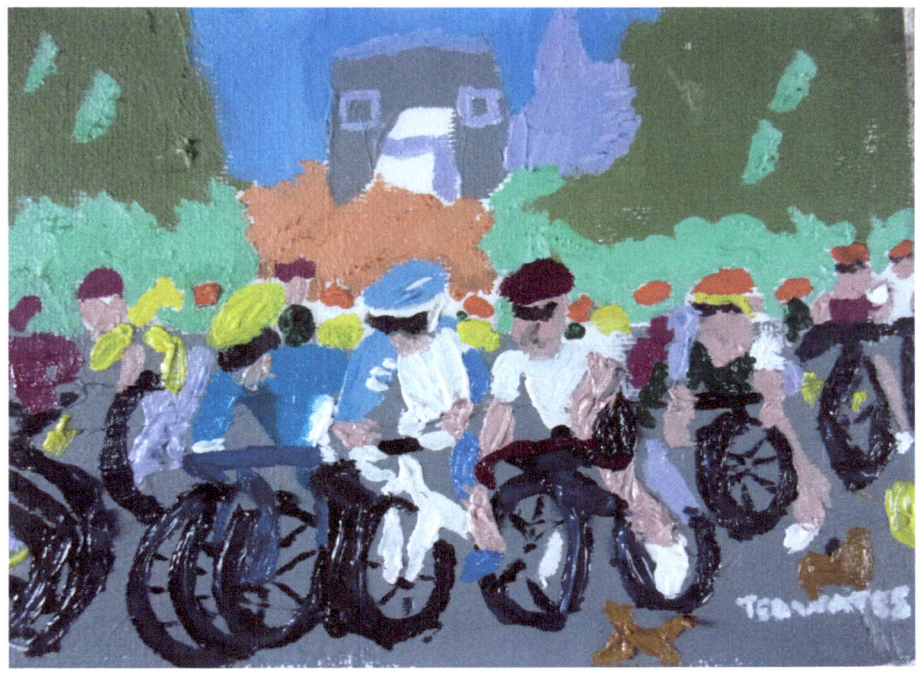

ABOVE: Tour de France (SOLD)

The colours and the activity all conspired to make me reach for my brushes on this occasion.

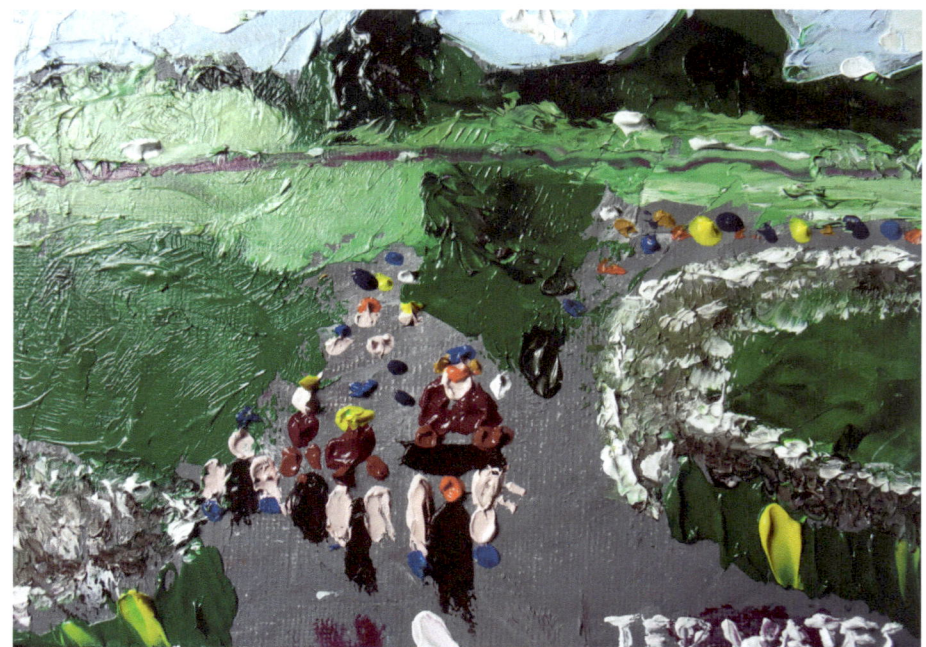

ABOVE: *Tour de Yorkshire*

I couldn't forget Yorkshire, could I? The scenery makes a nice contrast to France.

SKETCHBOOK

Ted loves his sketchbook. It's so easy to carry round and when there's time he just uses any pencil to hand whether it's an HB or 2B. He's not picky. He might be sitting on the settee, out in the garden or on holiday. Often his children will inspire him - their actions and joy of playing inspiring his next picture. Sketching is a great way of improving any ability Ted might have. Sometimes he might colour his doodles in and very occasionally they form the basis of his paintings. What follows is a little insight into Ted's cherished sketchbook.

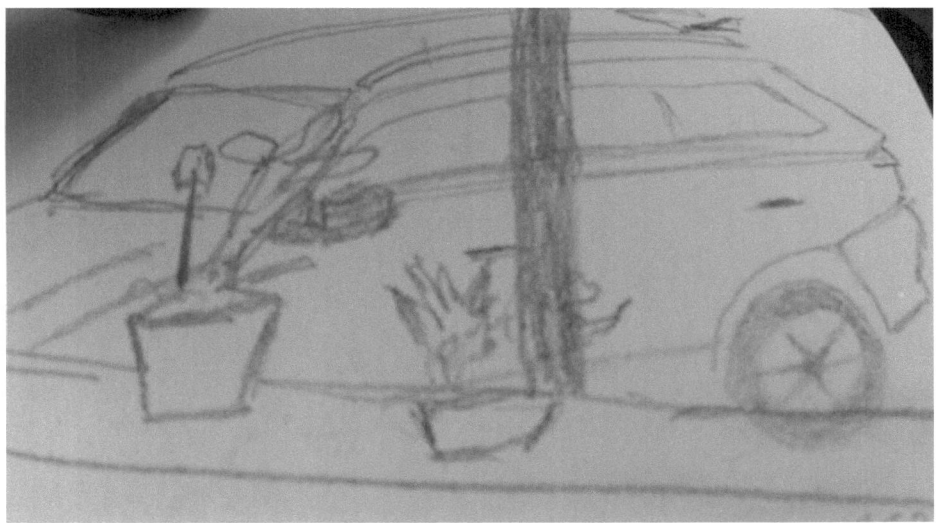

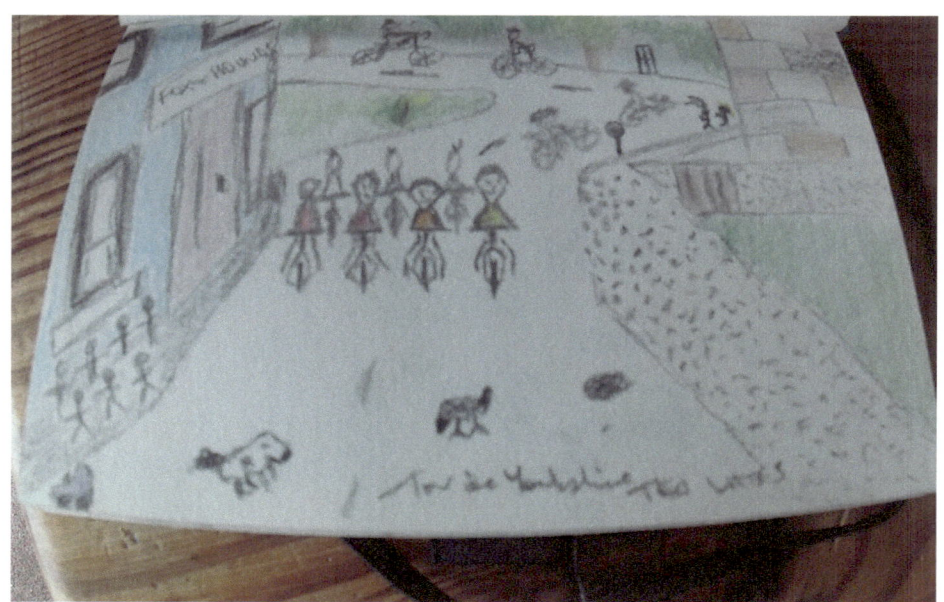

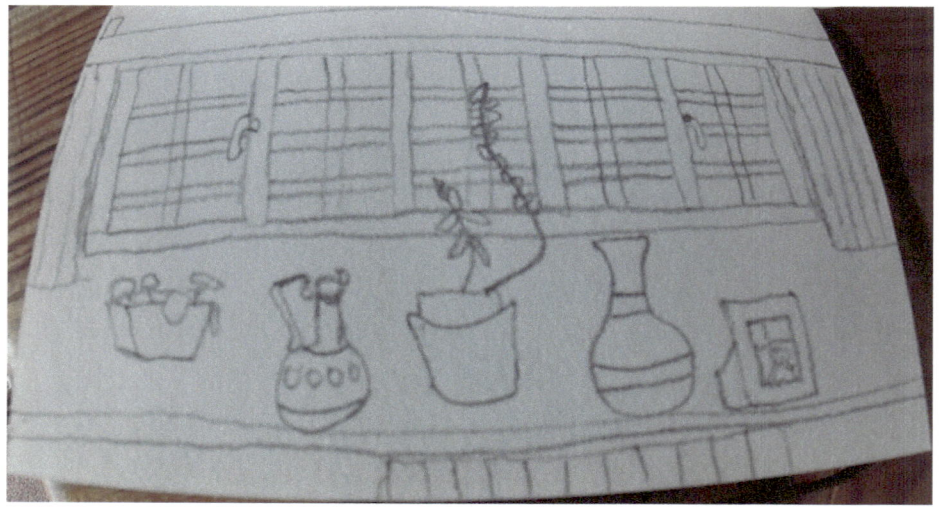

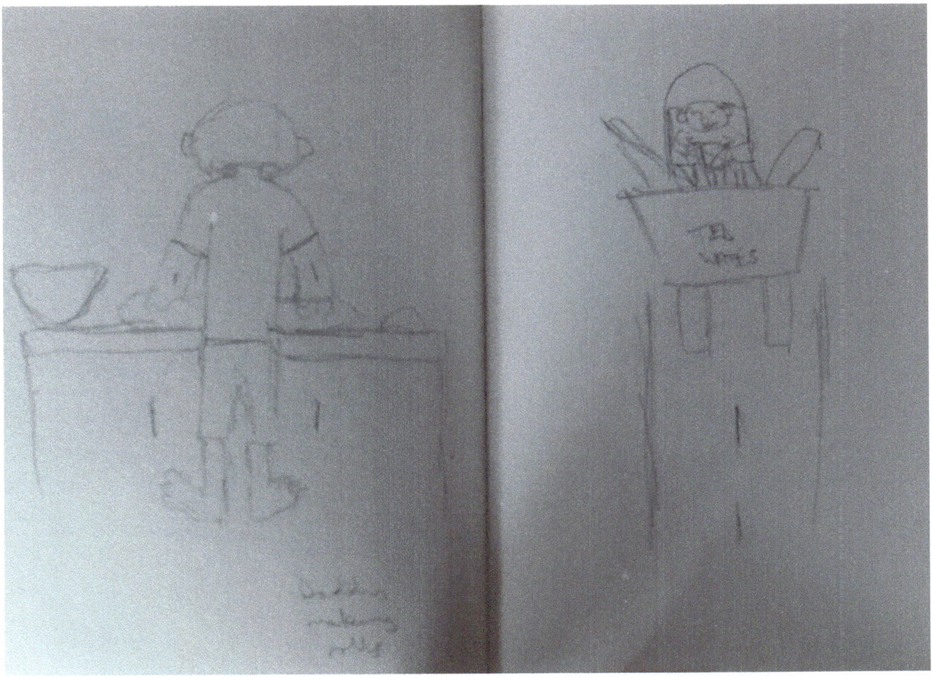

THE ART OF TED WATES

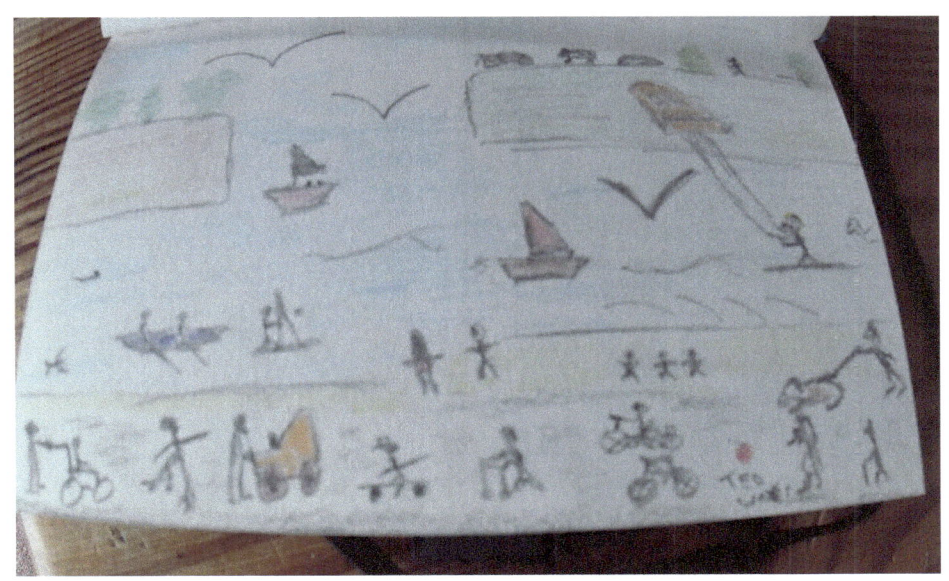

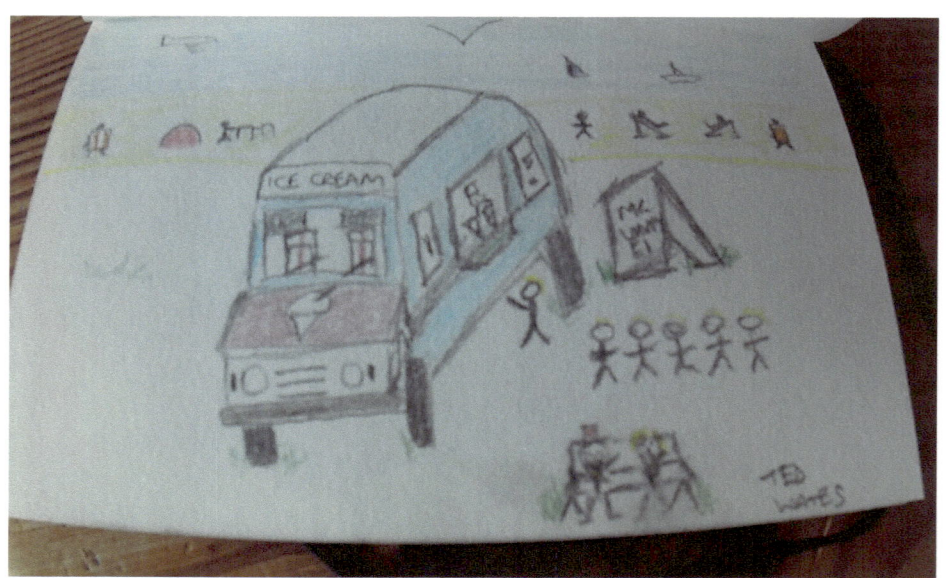

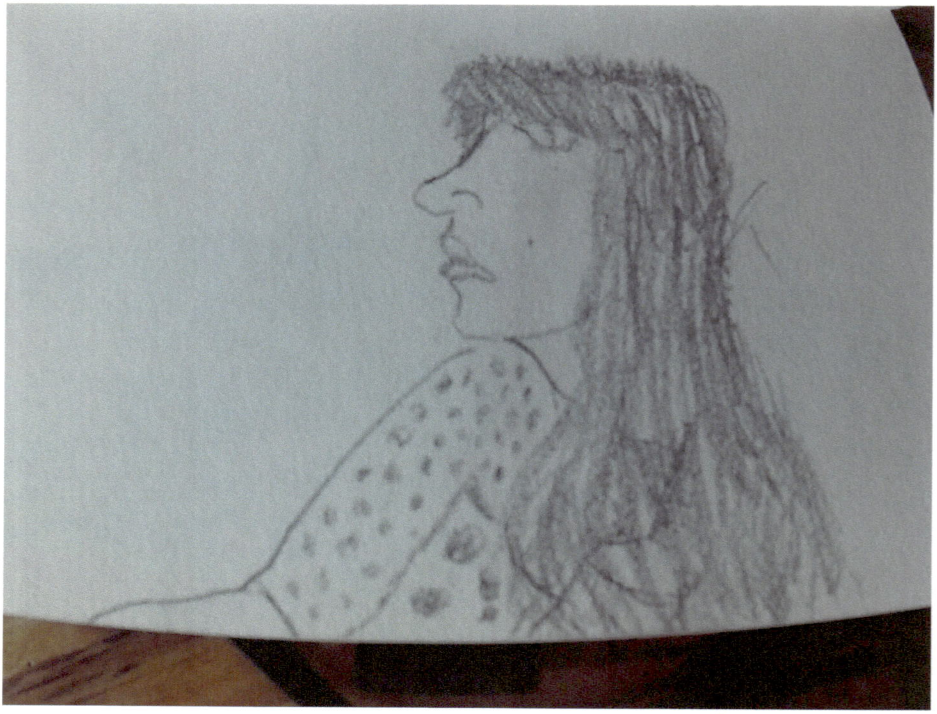

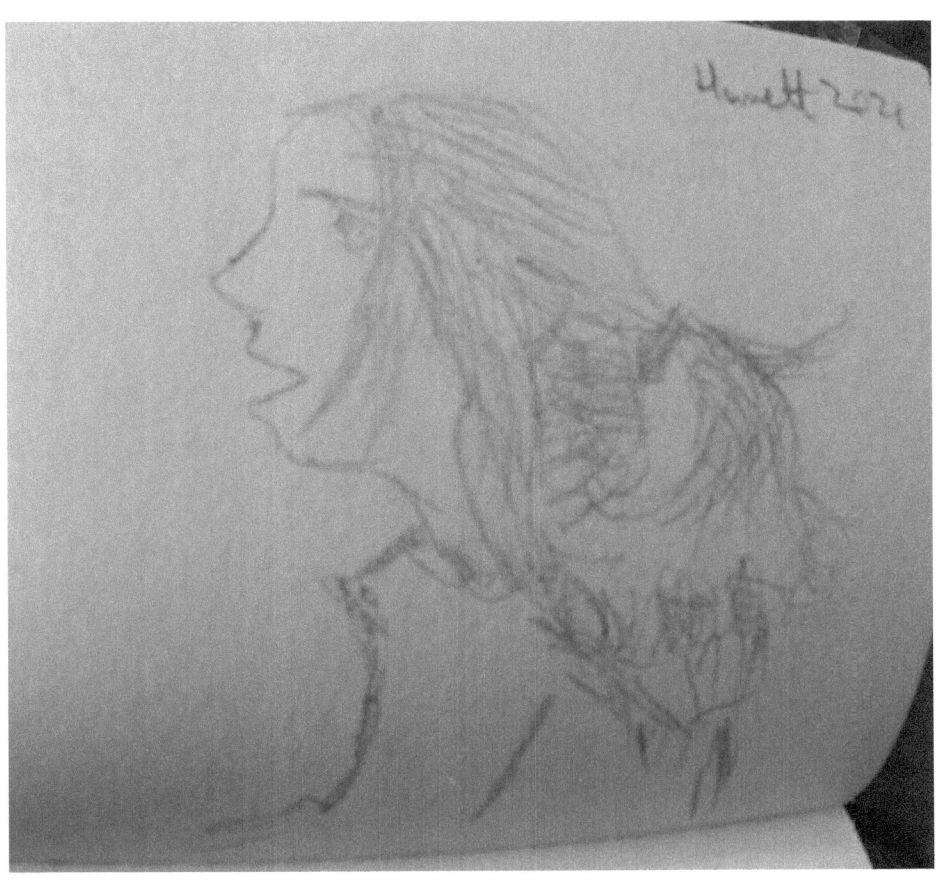

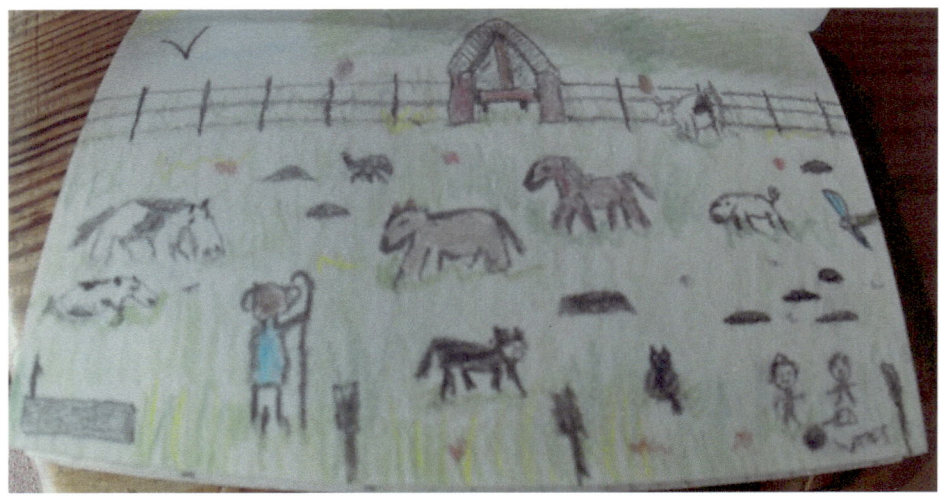
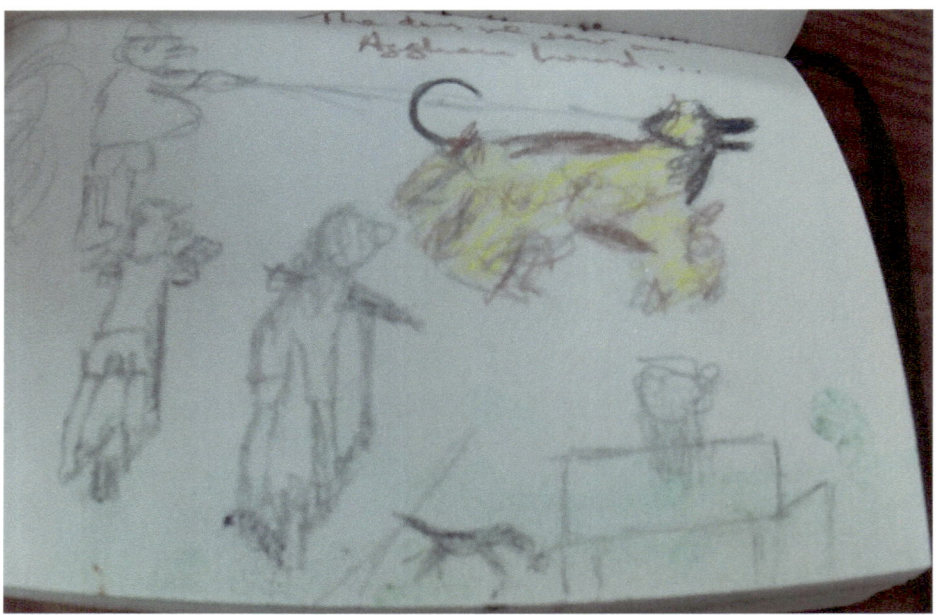

THE ART OF TED WATES

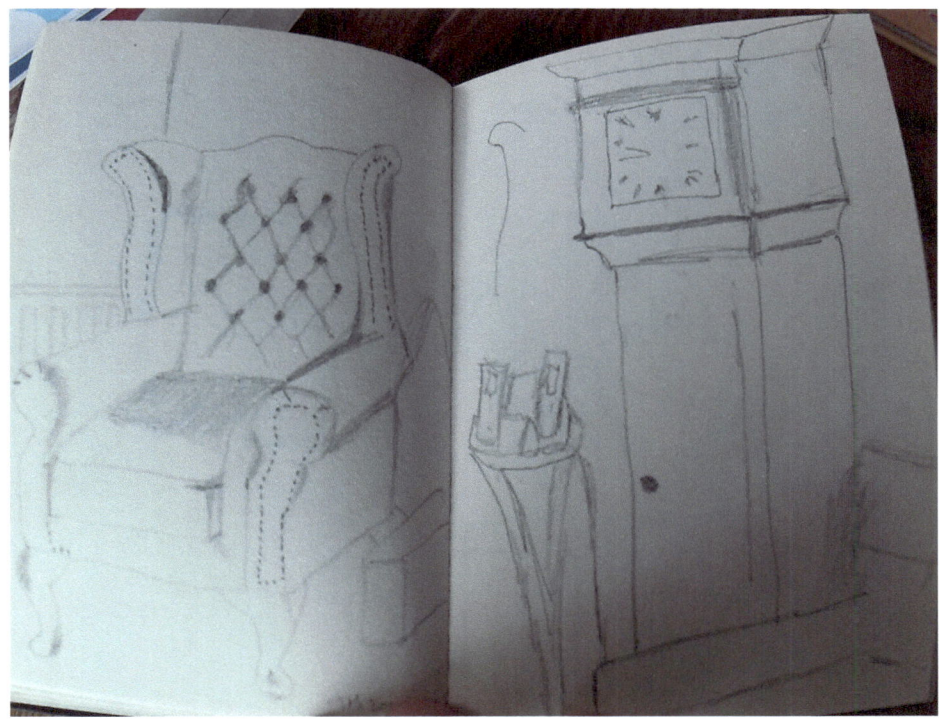

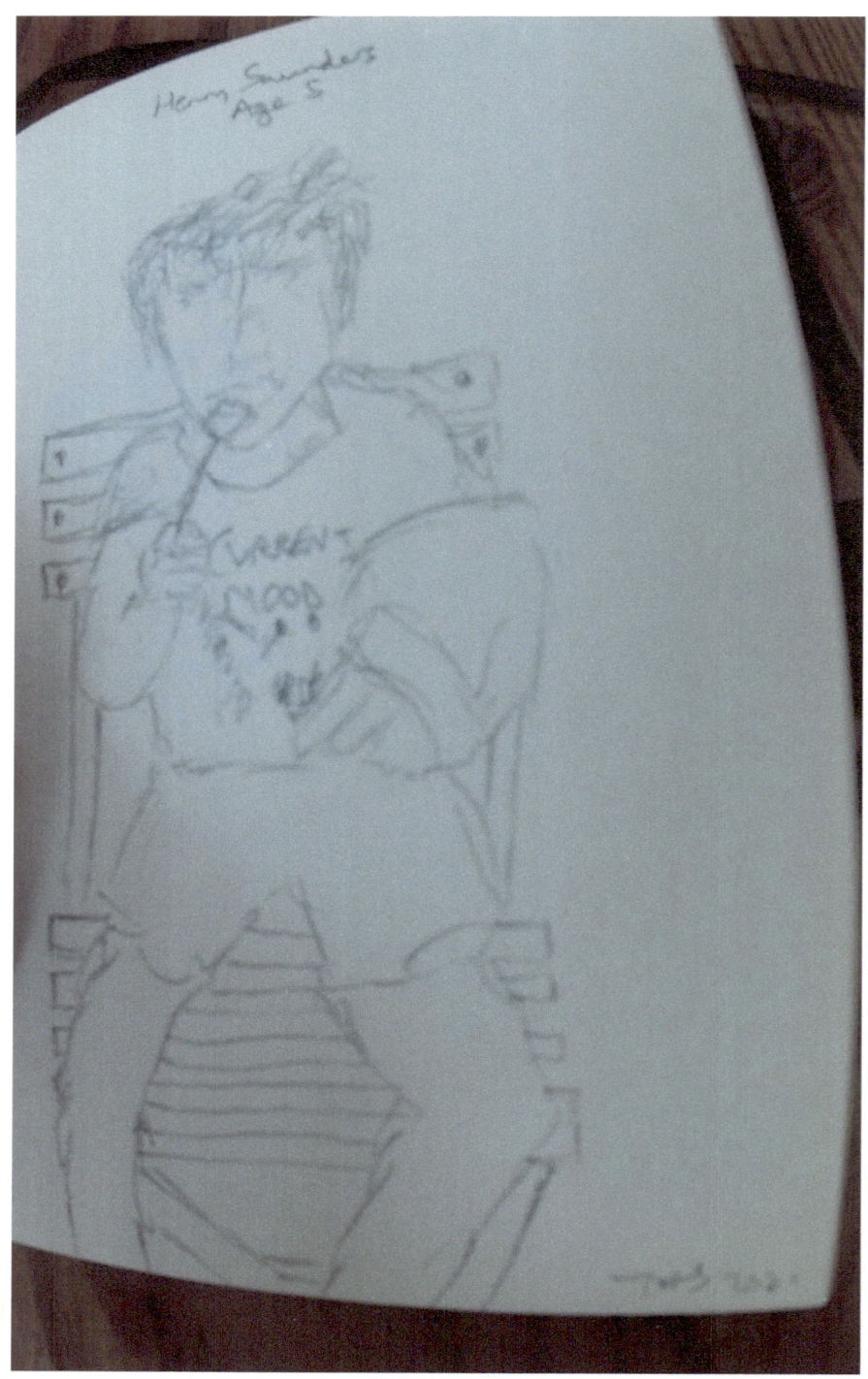

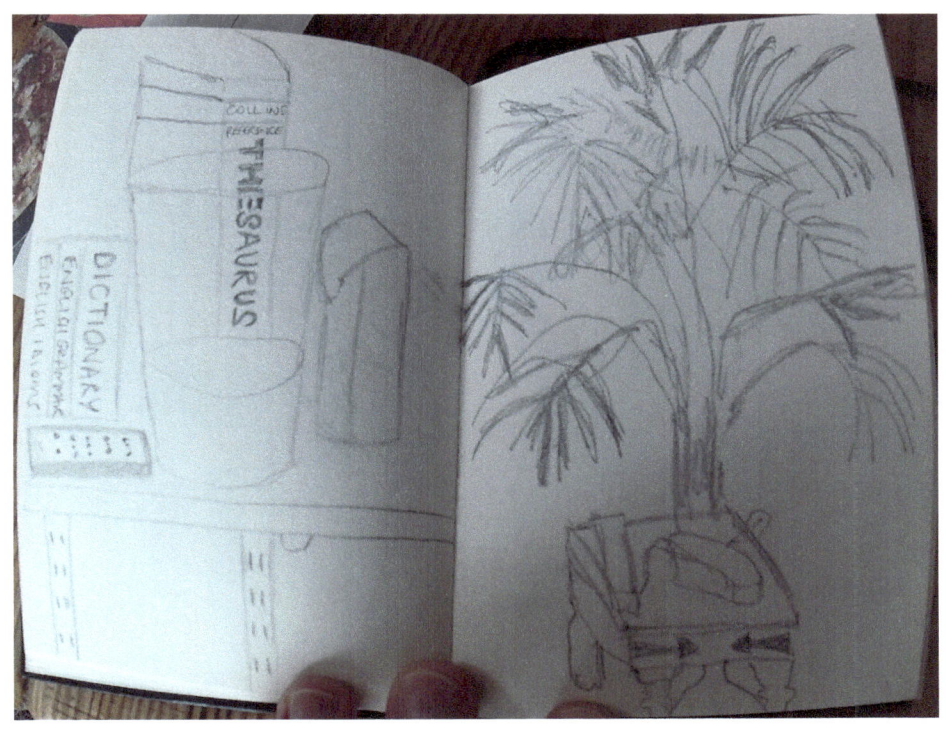

ABOUT THE AUTHOR

Tim Saunders

British journalist Timothy Alletson Saunders contributes to publications in England, America and New Zealand. He is publisher and editor of Contemporary Artist and hosts the In Conversation podcast.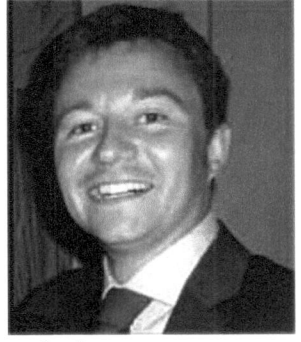
Since 2013 Tim and his wife Caroline have run creativecoverage.co.uk which handles marketing for selected professional artists and craftspeople. It also publishes books and websites.
As the poet TA Saunders he has written the following collections:

Poems for Today
The Early Years
Turbulent Times
Best Loved Poems
Life

He is the author of various books: A Book of Short Stories, Family Cars, Family Staycations, Photographs of the British Isles, A Touch of Celebrity, The Art of Ted Wates. His large format children's book is Eric the worm. Books Tim has been commissioned to write for other publishers are: The Essential Buyer's Guide to the BMW X5 (Veloce), Hampshire Living Memories (Francis Frith), Southampton's Heritage Revealed and Around Fareham Past and Present (both Sutton Publishing).
Tim is editor of Travel & motoring magazine. For a number of years he was business and motoring editor at the Bournemouth Daily Echo.

PRAISE FOR AUTHOR

Excellent colourful piece. Small size suits my wishes. Artist approachable and engaging, recommended.

- JONATHAN MATHER

TIM SAUNDERS PUBLICATIONS
memoir, art, poetry and more

"Everybody has a book in them," according to journalist Christopher Hitchens (1949 to 2011)

Do you have a book you would like to publish?

Email. tsaunderspubs@gmail.com

For more information visit:
tsaunderspubs.weebly.com

Unsolicited manuscripts welcome.

www.ingramcontent.com/pod-product-compliance
Lightning Source LLC
Chambersburg PA
CBHW040323220526
45473CB00009B/2545